Dead Towns

 of central and western Kansas

A collection of stories from **The Hutchinson News**

Written by Amy Bickel

❖❖❖

Written by Amy Bickel
Edited by Jason Probst
Cover photograph by Travis Morisse
Book design by Jim Heck

ISBN 978-0-9840005-0-0
Library of Congress Control Number: 2011941554

Printed in the U.S.A. by Mennonite Press, Inc., Newton, KS

First Printing

Preface

Today the "Dead Towns" of Kansas are little more than empty buildings, broken walls or wide spots along a state highway or county road. Few people drive through, and those who do might notice the remnants of a town or a village, but they're less likely to notice its former promise.

Like every prairie town, these, too, were places that were going somewhere. They had churches, lumberyards, general stores and concert halls. Some just needed the railroad to cut a path through their town. Others schemed to win the county seat – and a permanent place on the map – only to lose out to a neighboring city. Still, some simply faded away slowly as fewer families made their living from the land and children migrated away from the windswept plains to the opportunities that could be found in the city.

A few still cling to life today, with a handful of loyal residents or through the childhood memories of rural residents who remember what the town might have been. A generation will pass, however, and those towns likewise will fade into history and join the other dead or dying towns in Kansas.

Through the broken buildings and overgrown prairie grass, however, is a rich history and a story that's worth telling, and remembering.

It might be the cattle town of Trail City, on the Kansas-Colorado border, whose reputation for debauchery made Dodge City look tame by comparison. Or the battle for the Wichita County seat between Coronado and Leoti, which escalated to a bloody and deadly gunfight that made headlines in the New York Times and reportedly attracted the attention of Dodge City lawmen Bat Masterson and Wyatt Earp, along with Doc Holliday. And Carter Spur, a sordid little railroad stop at the intersection of Rice, Reno and McPherson Counties, where drunkenness and gambling were commonplace during the height of prohibition.

Hutchinson News reporter Amy Bickel spent nearly two years - 2010 and 2011 - researching the history of some of Central and Western Kansas' Dead Towns. The result was a weekly series that appeared in The News titled "Dead Towns." Readers responded with interest, curiosity and tips on other towns with glorious or notorious pasts, leading The News to compile the series for publication as a book.

We hope you'll find as much enjoyment in reading about Kansas' past as we found in researching and writing about it. Kansas has a rich and vivid history, full of stories about treachery, desperation, strength and hope – and much of it can be found in the stories behind Kansas' Dead Towns.

John D. Montgomery
Editor and publisher
The Hutchinson News

Dead towns

❖ of central and western Kansas

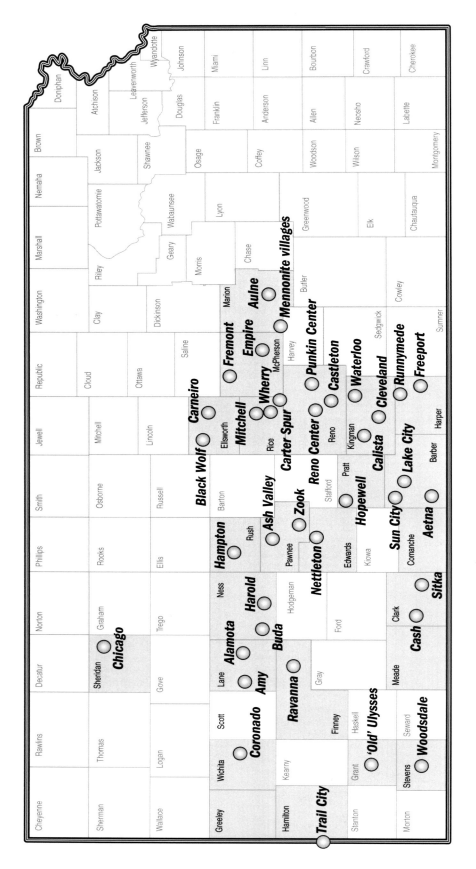

❖ The Towns ❖

Chicago

❖ Sheridan County ❖

It was named after the Illinois city because it was considered the busiest place in the county. Now the only traffic is farm trucks in this sparsely populated part of Sheridan County.

What remains is an old, deserted schoolhouse sandwiched between a couple of circles of irrigated corn on the plains of Sheridan County. The white paint is nearly gone. Warm prairie winds blow through cracks in the boarded-up windows, helping collect dust on what is inside – auditorium seats and trash, along with a broom that hasn't swept anything in decades.

A dilapidated home rests nearby. Outside, a rusty marker sticks up in the tall weeds – the only remnant giving this dead town a name.

Chicago.

It's a town forgotten as time marches on, a town named so because it was considered the busiest place in the county – a stagecoach stop where its residents had dreams of a thriving city. Yet, on a sultry summer day in 2010, Hutchinson resident Mark Nisly traveled the Kansas highways northwestward after hearing a story from a fellow in his local motorcycle group. The man said he had once stumbled upon Chicago, Kan., during a hunting excursion many years before.

This gave Prairie Pups Motorcycle Club members a goal. Nisly, who was the club's president at the time, suggested members should take a road trip to prove or disprove Chicago's existence.

Location: Chicago school is 1 ¼ miles west of the Lucerne Cemetery. A few other buildings are located south of the school.

On Aug. 13, after work at Nisly Business Consultants – his home-based company – the 53-year-old Nisly began his journey on his red Kawasaki motorcycle – not knowing where to look or even if there was anything to find.

"I was pretty sure, looking at Google images, that there wouldn't be anything there," Nisly said. "It looked like the crops were growing right next to the road."

Dying towns on the prairie

Across Kansas, there are at least 6,000 dead or dying towns, said former Kansan Dan Fitzgerald, author of "Faded Dreams: Ghost towns of Kansas," among other ghost town books.

Not unlike Chicago, these towns' founders had high hopes for their havens on the prairie: successful businesses lining the main street, a school full of children, clapboard houses painted in a sundry of colors.

Yet, if the railroad skirted a town, the dreams dampened, he said. It was the biggest cause of demise for many a town on the plains during the late 1800s. Later on, survival was dependent on highway systems, the agricultural economy and whether a community could keep a school – a vicious circle when it comes to rural exodus.

Some endured less than a decade, said Lyn Frederickson, head of reference at the Kansas State Historical Society. Others began to dwindle during the Great Depression.

"Kansas had boom and bust cycles," she said. "Towns for one reason or another grew rapidly then never maintained that population again."

A few of those towns on Fitzgerald's top 10 list:

Irving – The Marshall County town founded in 1859 didn't start off well. In May 1879, two tornadoes an hour apart decimated the town of 300, writes Fitzgerald. One destroyed the northern end, the other the southern end. Irving rebuilt, only to be abandoned in 1960, with the construction of Tuttle Creek Reservoir. Coincidently, Tuttle Creek never covered the town with water.

"You can walk the lonely streets, kick a few building foundation stones, even leave a message for future travelers in a mailbox set up toward the center of town," according to Fitzgerald.

Empire City – The Cherokee County town boomed in the 1870's due to mining and once had as many as 3,000 miners. The town declared war on nearby Galena, and "when the smoke cleared, the town went rapidly downhill as quickly as it boomed."

By 1910, much of the town was annexed to Galena. Some of the mineshafts and chat piles next to them still exist, as well as a few old buildings, Fitzgerald said.

Neosho Falls – It may be the state's most famous ghost town, since it inspired an album by the rock group, Kansas. Fitzgerald first found the town by accident in 1978, a town where people just walked away after the 1951 flood ravaged the community.

Chicago

Photo courtesy Mark Nisly

After he challenged members of his motorcycle club to find the ghost town of Chicago, Kan., Hutchinson resident Mark Nisly headed northwestward on a journey that took him 934 miles before he made it to the Sheridan County dot in the road.

"The hardware store had hardware on the shelves; town hall had a rotting stage with a rotting piano on the stage," Fitzgerald writes. "Sheet music blew in the breeze. One building, probably a general store, had antique furniture rotting away. The town school had pictures of the graduating class still hanging on the walls; even though everything was wide open and you could walk through it. The bank had a wide-open safe against one wall."

Unfortunately, after he mentioned the town in one of his books, folks began carting off artifacts. Still, he reports, there is much to see, including the old, vine-covered school.

Exodus continues

Other towns have similar stories. Remains of the Ravanna School and a former Garfield County courthouse rest in a Finney County field, along with a cemetery. The town lost the battle for the county seat to nearby Eminence, also a ghost town. State officials later deemed Garfield an illegal county due to its small acreage after being alerted by bitter Ravanna residents. Meanwhile, Kansas Pacific Railroad's plans to put in tracks from Ravanna to Dodge City did not come to fruition. All these things led to the end of this western Kansas town.

The Hamilton County town of Coolidge, population 86, also dwindled from its peak significantly, Fitzgerald said, noting the town might be too far from an epicenter to survive. Fitzgerald considers it already a ghost town, but adds in the next 20 years, other towns could meet similar situations as farms become larger, schools close and rural outmigration continues.

"Larger farms mean fewer people, and if (a town) loses its school, the lifeblood of the community, that can be a real killer," he said.

Some towns have taken the incentive to address issues, he said, noting that after he wrote about the Chautauqua County town of Elk Falls as a potential ghost town, city leaders became enraged enough to start making improvements, including adding an arts foundation.

The technology age could help some rural communities, he said, calling the Internet "the great rural leveler."

Yet, Fitzgerald said, he expects to see some cities continue spiraling downward – which was evident when the government released the 2010 census population figures this spring.

In all, 77 counties lost population between 2000 and 2010. Western Kansas counties took the biggest hit, with only seven counties in the western half of the state seeing an increase.

7

Chicago

"I'd like to say the process of dying off is over, but just in the last 30 years, some of these towns I go to over and over again still show signs of collapse," Fitzgerald said. "Unfortunately, I might have some more towns to write about in the next 20 or 30 years."

The busiest place in the county

These days, about the only thing that kicks up dusts around Chicago, Kan., is farmers driving trucks or farm machinery down the gravel roads on their way to plant crops or check fields. Sheridan County, after all, has a population of just 2,400 people, half of them living in the county seat of Hoxie.

"That area up there, it's basically no-man's land," said Marilyn Carder, with the Sheridan County Historical Society. "There's probably four miles there where you'd go without seeing a thing except fence rows and crops."

Nevertheless, 130 years ago, residents saw promise for their little neighborhood, even if it was short lived.

George M. Taylor began operating a post office, stagecoach stop and general store at Chicago on July 8, 1880, Carder said. During that time, Carder figures the one-room school was started, noting they don't have county records before 1897.

The town, however, never took off much more, she said. The post office closed on Oct. 18, 1887. The school closed in 1954. The neighborhood built a church, once located near the school, in 1910. It closed in the early 1960s. While the church no longer is standing, the school remains, as well as the abandoned home not far away.

This is what Nisly found when he made the journey. Arriving at Colby past dark on a Friday, he took a side trip into Colorado for a motorcycle gathering Saturday. There, he picked up Hutchinson resident Bill Massingill and the two traveled via their motorcycles back into Sheridan County on Sunday.

"I stopped in Atwood and a guy there didn't know anything about it," Nisly said of Chicago, but added he had an idea where to go from the Google map he found on the Internet.

Forty-six hours, two motel bills and 934 miles later, Nisly said he finally found the Chicago school surrounded in weeds, along with the old house guarded by a vulture. He snapped photos of his motorcycle with the buildings.

Nisly and Massingill also stopped by the ghost town of Lucerne, just four miles to the east. Remains include a cemetery, an old stone foundation and half a wood sign that once read Lucerne – the last four letters vaguely readable. The town had a post office from 1880 to 1943.

It didn't surprise Nisly that the towns died, noting there was no nearby railroad and the areas were more conducive to growing crops than towns.

Moreover, he said, the reason for the trip was to ride his motorcycle, to get off the beaten path and see something new.

"I must admit, I enjoyed my trip to Chicago, Kansas, much more than my recent trip to Chicago, Illinois," he said.

An early photo of Chicago shows a church and school buildings.

Auditorium seating and a broom still remain in the inside of the old school that closed in the 1950's.

Greeley County

❖ Colokan * Astor * Horace * Hector * Greeley Center * Chappaquq * Whitelaw ❖

"Go West," Horace Greeley exclaimed. But Greeley County towns tied to historic New York newspaperman died long ago.

It has been more than 150 years since the New York newspaperman told easterners to "Go West."

Yet, in Greeley County, Horace Greeley's name lives on. The county seat is named after his newspaper. The county and a town both carry his name. There are ghost towns, as well, influenced by the New York Tribune publisher, including the communities of Whitelaw and Reid – named after an editor – and Hector, after his dog.

In 1841, Greeley established the Tribune, which became the leading national newspaper of its time. He helped form the Republican Party and, as an abolitionist, he fought for Kansas' entry into the Union as a free state. Greeley ran against Ulysses S. Grant in 1872 for the presidency, but lost, dying before the votes were even counted.

Still, Greeley's devotees named towns, streets and counties after him. That included W.C. Gerard. Gerard founded Tribune in 1885, which was originally known as Chappaqua and located a mile north of present-day Tribune. However, the name changed shortly after its founding.

"He was never out here," Nadine Cheney, curator of the Horace Greeley Museum, said of the county's namesake.

Yet people like Gerard coming from the east were largely influenced by Greeley and his newspaper.

Ghost towns of Greeley County

County settlers had dreams of westward expansion populating their county.

Located far west on the Colorado border, Greeley County was the last Kansas county to incorporate. Pioneers came for farmland offered for the taking through the government. The railroad was selling land. They began to till the land using oxen and horses. These folks lived in sod houses and started towns as commerce centers, hoping their community would become the new county's county seat.

For instance, four miles north of Horace there was Hector, named after Horace Greeley's dog. In April 1886, C.T. Thompson began publishing the Hector Echo, Cheney said. Hector also had had two hotels, two stage lines, a lumberyard, hardware store, a land-and-loan company and good water.

In December 1885, Hector got a post office. A newspaper chronicling the blizzard of 1886 reported that newly named postmaster, George Chapman, didn't assume his post, as he died in the blizzard. Even with all of these new businesses, in

the summer and fall of 1886, the town of Hector declined and was transplanted to Tribune. It became the first ghost town in Greeley County as a result, according to Fort Hays State University.

Greeley Center, a town north and west of present day Horace, was the county's second ghost town. Named after Horace Greeley, the Greeley Town Co. formed Greeley Center in October 1885, according to Fort Hays.

The community had a newspaper, the Greeley County Gazette, edited by the Wilbe brothers from Hutchinson, Cheney said. There also was the Greeley House Hotel, a livery stable, a grocery store, blacksmith, general store, lumberyard and drugstore.

Cheney said the newspaper reported 75 new arrivals in one day's time. However, in June 1887, the boom ended.

Settlers had already started the town of Horace in 1886 and Greeley Center lost a significant number of businesses to Horace, Fort Hays reported. By June 1887, the Denver, Memphis and Atlantic Railroad put tracks through Horace and left Greeley Center unable to continue its growth.

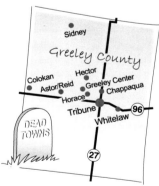

"The last remnants of Greeley Center were plowed and cleared away by 1894, never to be seen again," according to Fort Hays. "A lot of the buildings moved to Horace, all planning on being by the railroad tracks. But they did not come through Hector and they did not come through Greeley Center."

On the Colorado/Kansas line

While Colokan didn't have a tie to Horace Greeley, it was settled by those seeking land to the east. It was located just off the Colorado/Kansas border, not far from the Colorado community of Towner.

According to Fort Hays, Civil War veterans from Illinois came and settled in Greeley County, forming what was known as a soldiers' colony. In 1887, the colony merged with the United Presbyterian colony, forming Colokan Town Co. The

Greeley County

A photo dated between 1900 and 1905 shows children with a ball and croquet equipment in front of a sodhouse in Greeley County.

A photo dated between 1880 and 1890 in Greeley County shows two children informally posed with their mules. For many students in the 1880's and the 1910's, the commute to school consisted of walking.

first issue of the newspaper, the Colokan Graphic, edited by O.Q. McNeil, was published in October 1887, Cheney said. It advertised Robert Rockwell's new hotel and restaurant with meals at any hour.

Colokan had a real estate office, notary public, a grocery and a blacksmith. The Denver, Memphis and Atlantic Railroad went through the town and the town of Towner. However, when Towner got the depot instead of Colokan, the latter folded.

By 1897, the town had been completely vacated and little remains today of what once was known as "The Star of Western Kansas," according to Fort Hays. Not far away is the Rogers Cemetery, Cheney said. It's where two Rogers brothers were buried, along with their faithful collie, after dying in the blizzard of 1886. She said there are 57 graves there, and volunteers try to maintain it several times a year.

Whitelaw and Reid

Whitelaw Reid was an editor at the New York Tribune and a close friend to Greeley. He was on Republican incumbent Benjamin Harrison's presidential ticket as the vice president, although the duo lost.

Thus, two towns are named after the man – Whitelaw and Reid. Whitelaw had a post office from 1888 to 1890, according to the Kansas State Historical Society. And Cheney said it had an elevator and a few houses. Residents at Reid, however, had bigger dreams. Thinking it would be the county seat, the newspaper in Tribune moved to the newly formed town of Reid in 1887.

The railroad line went 2½ miles west of Greeley Center, which ultimately became the site of Reid. The town had 50 residents in June 1887. Old Tribune, before the county seat election, eventually moved a mile south to catch the railroad, helping secure its place in the present day. In November 1888, Tribune was declared the county seat over Horace and Reid, with 420 votes in favor of Tribune, 202 votes in favor of Horace, and only 2 votes going to Reid.

When Tribune became the county seat, all the businesses from the different towns began to move their stores to Tribune, Cheney said. The moving of these businesses ulti-

mately led to the demise of Reid. In 1891, there were 26 people living in Reid, now called Astor by those residents. By 1897, the town became a ghost town and the town company eventually sold the land for $35.01 in 1901 to pay the back taxes on it. Locals probably named Astor after John Jacob Astor, one of the richest men in the 19th century. Horace Greeley was a critic of the New Yorker, and a Greeley County illustrated map from 1897 depicts a man with dollar signs on his head.

"Reid/Astor faded into the Kansas background just like so many other settlements of the time period," Fort Hays reported. Other towns tried to start, as well, including Ainsworth, Thelma, Locust, Youngsville, Hurt and Sidney. Each had a post office, but none of the towns lasted much past the 20th century.

Two towns remain

Except for Horace and Tribune, the county's only incorporated cities, nothing remains of any of these ghost towns, Cheney said. Cheney has trekked through every town site in the county, finding only fragments of life. There are a few foundations at Astor. She has found broken glass, pieces of concrete and square nails.

"Wherever man goes, he leaves trash," she said. Moreover, the county never saw the populations it did when these towns were thriving.

The 1890 census shows the county population at more than 2,600 inhabitants in 1887, according to "Kansas: A Cyclopedia of State History." It is unclear whether the county actually had that many people. Census numbers show dramatic drops after that, including just 1,200 people in 1890, and the population in 1900 dipped below 500 people. In 2009, the U.S. Census estimated the county had 1,200 people – the smallest in Kansas.

It didn't take long for early day farmers to realize that growing crops in the semiarid terrain wasn't easy. Some moved to Holly, Colo., Cheney said. Others went elsewhere.

"Some of them left for the Oklahoma (land) run," she said. "Many times they couldn't find water in Greeley County, and they seemed to move on."

Trail City

❖ Hamilton County ❖

The town on the Kansas/Colorado state line was once considered the wickedest little town in the west.

It's against the law for a woman to ride naked on a horse through Coolidge.

Or, at least, that's the story Larue Lennen tells – a story passed down from her mother, a former mayor of Coolidge – a town just a few miles from the Kansas border.

When an unclothed prostitute from the rough border town of Trail City came riding into Coolidge, residents decided they wanted to make sure it never happened again. Trail City, after all, was the notorious stepchild of the area – a place of gambling and drinking, of womanizing and, on occasion, of murder. It was a town without a county or state, for that matter – a city located in what locals dubbed a "No Man's Land," Larue Lennen said.

So disorderly was this town that for years after its death locals wouldn't talk about it, maybe because their men sometimes sneaked over to visit.

Larue Lennen, however, along with her daughter, Lori, is on a mission to preserve the history – working on a document that tells the tale.

"Otherwise," Larue Lennen said. "These stories will all be lost."

Cattle, liquor and women

Trail City, known as the "Wickedest little town on the Arkansas River," as well as the "Hellhole on the Arkansas," grew because the Kansas Legislature prohibited Texas ranchers from driving their herds across the Kansas prairie to market because the cattle carried Texas fever, which was caused by ticks. With no railroads yet on the Texas plains, the only way to move cattle was through towns like Ellsworth, Abilene and Dodge City, according to the book, "Hamilton County, Kansas History."

While the cattle were immune to the fever themselves, the infection could spread to domestic livestock. The governor officially signed the quarantine law in 1885.

Martin Culver, a Texas rancher and a large dealer in Corpus Christi, Texas, had the first herd to encounter the boycott. When his herds reached Kansas, they were met by Kansas guards who informed crews they could no longer cross into the state. Thus, the herdsmen were forced to go westward and then travel up the western edge of Kansas, which became known as the National Cattle Trail, according to the book.

Culver, among others, petitioned Washington for a strip of land three miles wide that separated Kansas and Colorado. This "no man's land" would be away for cattle to go up to Montana. Lori Lennen said future president Teddy Roosevelt was a proponent of the new trail, as he purchased many of the cattle that came up from Texas for his Montana ranch.

Thus, Culver, a trail promoter, developed the town of Trail City with $20,000 in capital stock, situating the "cowboy capital" on the state line, moving his family to Coolidge in 1884. Businesses began to pop up. According to the Prowers County Historical Society, with the town on the Colorado-Kansas border, buildings on the east side of the street had back doors that opened into Kansas.

"This afforded much hilarity in the saloons on the east side of the street as bottles were tossed into dry Kansas," according to the Prowers County website.

Trail City survived for a time because of the trail. Cattlemen drove the herds under the railroad bridge at Cheyenne Creek, which was a few hundred yards west of the state line, according to the Coolidge history book. The cattle went under the bridge two by two, with Culver assessing a tax per animal.

Location: Trail City is located on the Kansas/Colorado state line, just south of U.S. Highway 50. A trail road takes visitors to the former town site.

Lori Lennen said she has found the tax to be between 2 and 10 cents a head and the Coolidge history book states it was 50 cents a head.

Yet, it was the other activity that occurred at Trail City that had people, including those in nearby Coolidge, talking.

To some, according to the book "History of Coolidge, Kansas," Trail City "made old Dodge City look like a Sunday school picnic."

It was one of the first stops on the trail for these cowboys, many who were paid just $30 a month, Lori Lennen said.

Trail City

Amy Bickel/The Hutchinson News

Trail City survived for a time because of the National Cattle Trail. Cattlemen drove the herds under the railroad bridge at Cheyenne Creek, which was a few hundred yards west of the state line. The cattle went under the bridge two by two, with a tax assessed at between 2 and 10 cents a head.

When they rode into Trail City, they didn't seem to mind spending their money at the various saloons or for a stint at one of the brothels.

"They'd charge (the cowboys) $10" for sex, Lori Lennen said with a laugh, noting the cowboys didn't seem to blink an eye at the cost – sometimes just signing up for the job because they wanted to get to Trail City.

"That would have been a lot of money back then," she said.

Culver, a tanner, had a shop where he sold saddles and other items, Lori Lennen said. He also constructed a hotel and had a saloon.

Another man, Print Olive, built a large stable and wagon yard. Joe Sparrow had another saloon, which was the rowdiest place in town, according to the Hamilton County history book.

In all, Trail City had about 250 permanent residents, but it would grow to nearly 500 when cowboys and transients came to town, according to a document Lennen provided. Moreover, with that many cowboys drinking and having sex, life here was raucous.

According to the Prowers County website, Trail City did have some law enforcement. However, "Being on the line between the two states, known as No-Man's Land, many of the criminals crossed the line into Kansas."

Several murders occurred during Trail City's short period, Lennen said. A document she read said one man visiting town reported seven murders in the short time he stayed at the city. The town marshal eventually died, as well as Print Olive, a murderer himself who was said to have been shot by saloon owner Joe Sparrow.

According to the Hamilton County history book, the act was a "brutal cold-blooded affair brought on by an old grudge and the refusal of Sparrow to pay a small bill which he owed."

Sparrow was twice found guilty. However, retried in Pueblo, he was found innocent. Meanwhile, National Cattle Trail founder Culver died in 1887 at age 47 from a ruptured appendix, according to one account. He is buried in Coolidge Cemetery, his burial plot marked by a cross tombstone.

No matter, Trail City's days were numbered. Trail-driving cattle was on the decline as some began to protest the tax, taking their cattle west. In addition, by this time, railroads shipped cattle rather than a herd of cowboys on horses, Lennen said.

Trail City's population was just 100 in 1887, according to documents. The 1888 Colorado Business Directory listed Trail City as having a railroad station, stage stop, post office and a population of 50. However, in 1889, the railroad stop and post office were gone, although the population was still 50.

By the early 1890s, locals moved many of the buildings to farms, to Holly, Colo., or into Coolidge, Lori Lennen said.

As for the graves of the men who died there, the Lennens aren't sure where Trail City folks buried the dead. It's possible that some of the graves at Coolidge Cemetery might have a few of the rough and tough cowboys.

Preserving history

On a chilly March evening, Lori Lennen walked around the old town site of Trail City, which is not far off of U.S. 50 on the south side of the road. Looking south, one can almost envision the roaring herds of cattle that once passed by here by the thousands.

These days, only a few limestone foundations stick up on the semiarid terrain. Impressions in the dirt show where basements or dugouts once sat and the railroad bridge still stands a few hundred yards down the tracks. The creek here is barely flowing and much of the bridge's supports are buried in silt.

On the Kansas side of the line, an old, stone home still stands, Lori Lennen saying early Trail City resident Glenn Jones once owned it.

Back on the highway is an old cafe/gas station, but that came decades after Trail City's heyday. Lennen even worked there as a waitress, she said with a chuckle.

Later that evening, Larue and Lori Lennen sat at their kitchen table, sifting through the information they had found

Trail City

over the past seven months on both Coolidge and Trail City. They've visited museums in both Kansas and Colorado, as well as the Kansas State Historical Society.

Lennen frequents both her home in Arizona and her mother's home in Coolidge. She talked about her dreams for the area, which includes marking the town and retelling its history that many have forgotten.

Even a nearby rest area just across the line into Colorado doesn't mention the wicked town that would have been less than 100 yards away.

History, too, is somewhat unclear, with the Lennens finding different accounts of the town in the research. During its heyday, even reporters didn't dare go to the town to write about it, she said, noting they were afraid of getting shot.

She owns a Trail City saloon, which was moved to Coolidge in 1887 and still stands. It was once a residence, but Lennen decided to turn it into a bed and breakfast. She began construction in March 2011 on the five-bedroom establishment, which, at the time, she said would be ready for visitors by fall.

"It was literally the lawless that lived here," she said. "It's a wonderful story."

Coronado

❖ Wichita County ❖

The wrinkled front of grim-visaged war in Wichita County has been veiled, and the authorities are counting the prisoners and casualties.
– New York Times, March 10, 1887

For decades, the 140-some-year-old single-shot Marlin OK Derringer was buried beneath the ground along a trail road between farm fields.

While walking through the area with his father, Jeff, and brother, Evan, on the opening day of pheasant season in November 2010, 11-year-old Aaron Ridder saw something sticking up from the dirt. His find might not seem unusual along the Kansas prairie – an old gun issued between 1863 and 1870 that settlers could have carried on their journeys west.

Except, that is, for its proximity to the Wichita County ghost town of Coronado.

Go back to Feb. 27, 1887, on what had been a quiet Sunday afternoon – when the men and henchmen supporting Leoti as the county seat came riding into Coronado. And, more than a century later, what happened that day is known as one of the bloodiest county seat wars in the American West.

A bloody battle

Many a county in Kansas was involved in a county seat battle. Only a few, however, involved death.

Wichita County Museum Curator Karen Walk said it's a story that most in the area have heard since grade school – an event told differently by both sides, making her wonder which story is true.

Both Leoti and Coronado were platted in 1885, just 2½ miles apart. Both towns grew rapidly, according to Walk. Residents erected businesses, houses and hotels. The founders of both towns had a dream their town would become the county seat.

"A bitter strife developed based on mutual efforts to secure the vital county seat," she wrote in an article about the event.

For several weeks, the editors of each town's newspaper wrote editorials bashing the other community and promoting the qualities of their own town. Leoti sent for "thugs" from Wallace to help with its effort.

On Feb. 8, 1887, a fraudulent temporary election took place with many votes bought at $50 a head. Voting lists also were filled with nonresident and fictitious voter names. Many people were intimidated and kept away from the polling spots by the "hired cowboys and thugs," Walk said.

Leoti became the temporary county seat, with the official election slated for March 10. Then, on Feb. 27, seven Leoti men jumped into a buckboard wagon with liquor and rifles and headed to Coronado for a little fun, Walk said. Someone eventually fired a shot and the battle began with Coronado men firing rounds of bullets from upper windows and doorways. A few victims fell from the wagon into the street.

Of the Leoti party, Charlie Coulter, an ex-Quantrill raider, William Rains and George Watkins were killed instantly, according to Walk. Two of the men escaped with the runaway team. Someone shot another man, Frank Jenness, six times. He died later.

"Albert Boorey was so riddled with bullets, it was a miracle he lived," she wrote. "A.R. Johnson lay on the street with a bullet in the head. Emmet Denning was hit in the leg and injured so badly it was later amputated."

No one from Coronado died, she said. Townsfolk in Leoti could hear the gunfire nearly 3 miles away.

The Coronado Herald reported the war in its newspaper with this spin:

When (the men from Leoti) arrived at Coronado, they proceeded to make everybody they met drink with them and tried to make a sick man get out of bed and dance at the muzzles of pistols. Later, Coulter commenced to knock men down with his pistol, while Frank Jenness would single out men to cover with his pistol. But such sport was too timid for drunken desperadoes so Coulter opened the ball by shooting Charles Loomis twice, while Rains shot him (Loomis) in the arm. Up to this time not a single weapon was drawn by a Coronado man, but after these three shots were fired by Coulter and Rains, it seemed for thirty seconds from pistol reports, that every man in and near the crowd was shooting. When the smoke cleared away, the old maxim was verified: Death loves a shining mark, and in Coulter and Rains it certainly had struck two daisies.

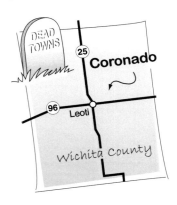

Location: About three miles east of Leoti on Kansas Highway 96.

Coronado

Wichita County Historical Society

A few famous cowboys helped battle it out in the Leoti/Coronado county seat fight. However, some historians question whether some of the famed lawmen actually were in the area. Nonetheless, according to the Museum of the Great Plains at Leoti, standing from left is Luke Short, Wyatt Earp, three unknown men, Doc Holliday, Bat Masterson, Bill Tilghman, Red Loomis, Jim Masterson and Pat and Mike Sughrue.

Meanwhile, the Leoti Standard had a different take on the story:

Coronado had been satisfied until Sunday to carry on the fight by trickery, fraud, lies and forgery, and, in this way, had managed to make the town and people despised by all who had the slightest insight into the matter. A note was placed in Mr. Coulter's hands on Sunday, inviting him over that afternoon and telling him to bring a friend or two with him and have a good time. It had been customary to visit back and forth, so in the afternoon the crowd of seven went over. ... After a couple of hours of pleasant chatting with their friends and acquaintances, they all got in the buggy and started off. As they drove by the bank building Frank Lilly, standing in front of the bank, applied some foul name to Mr. Rains, at the same time making a motion as if to draw a gun. Rains sprang from the buggy and said that Lilly would have to fight for that. Lilly replied that he had no gun, where upon Rains handed his gun to one of the party in the buggy and offered to fight with his fists. Lilly refused and Rains took his revolver and returned it to his pocket.

Charles and 'Red' Loomis and John Knapp were standing near the bank at the time. As Rains put up his gun, he remarked that he could easily whip Lilly. Lilly retaliated by calling him a liar, at which Rains drew his revolver and struck him over the head, mashing his hat, but not knocking him down. The men in ambush who were awaiting the signal now opened a volley of some sixty or seventy-five guns on the unsuspecting crowd (from

Leoti). Every man was shot; shot from the back. The four men on the ground were brought down and, of the three in the buggy, Watkins and Jenness fell out. After falling from the buggy Jenness got on his feet and started toward Leoti on a run. A number of shots were fired at him, five taking effect.

The incident made The New York Times on March 2, 1887, with the paper stating that Coronado was on guard in anticipation of an attack to avenge the deaths of the men killed. Lawmen from Dodge City came to Coronado after the fight to provide protection.

Among them, Walk said, were supposedly famed gunfighters Doc Holliday, Bat Masterson and Wyatt Earp. While a photo shows them among a group posing in front of Coronado's bank, some historians say this claim is inaccurate. One historian, Robert K. DeArment, who wrote the book "Bat Masterson: The Man and the Legend" wrote that Masterson thought the fears were unfounded and didn't put in an appearance in Wichita County.

Nevertheless, some of the men who were there may also have intimidated voters at the polls. Farmer City, located between the towns, hoped perhaps to secure the seat because of the feud.

However, on March 10, another county seat election named Leoti the permanent winner.

Walk said 21 Coronado men went to trial in Great Bend for murder. The towns had such conflicting stories of the incident that all the men were acquitted.

Coronado

The rest is history, Walk said. It didn't take long for the two towns to forget the past, with Leoti offering free town lots to Coronado residents. Soon, Coronado was just a memory on the prairie.

Walk tends to believe the Coronado paper has a little more truth to the story.

"It might have been fun to be a little mouse in the corner – to know all the details, and which stories are really true," she said. "I would like to know more of the real facts. You can assume and think and wonder about things, but really not knowing what really happened."

This old photo shows men and horses working along the railroad track at Coronado, now a ghost town 2½ miles east of Leoti. Arthur L. Walk is sitting on the rail.

Aaron said the gun is only about five inches in length – a single-shot pistol meant to be concealed, such as in a sleeve.

"It was pretty exciting," Aaron said, adding that Leoti resident Ray Grusing helped them identify the weapon.

Grusing, who served as the Wichita County sheriff in the late 1970s, is a gun collector. He took the gun home and looked through his books, finding an exact match.

He said from his findings that it was the only gun to have a pin in a certain spot in which the lever pivoted. The fact it is a concealed-type gun

Just a few artifacts

Nothing is left of the town site of Coronado except for a cemetery not far away.

Only a few tombstones remain, said Jeff Ridder, and only one stone is legible.

Walk figures that within 10 years of the county seat war, Coronado was nonexistent. Over the years, residents have found a few artifacts, including nails and glass. Some have found a few bricks from Coronado's old brick plant with the name "Coronado" printed on them.

Whether the old, rusted, bent gun was part of the battle or even from the days of Coronado is anyone's guess, said Ridder, whose farmland butts up against the Coronado town site. The fact Aaron found the gun within a half-mile of the area makes Ridder wonder.

found near Coronado makes it even more interesting.

However, he said, the monetary value isn't much. He told Aaron to hang on to his artifact.

"I praise that young man for finding it and not yielding it or turning it over to somebody," he said. "The fact he found it himself, and we know Coronado and Farmer City and Leoti had that fight – it could have very well been part of that."

The family keeps the gun in a safe, Jeff Ridder said, adding he was amazed by the discovery.

"I told him it was probably from when Coronado was here," he said. "I told him it was really old.

"It has been kind of neat," Jeff Ridder said. "Aaron has a renewed interest in treasure hunting. He wants to get a good metal detector."

From the New York Times, March 2, 1887

GARDEN CITY, Kan., March 2 –Ten cowboys armed to the teeth, and a posse of 20 citizens have been patrolling the streets of Coronado all day in anticipation of an attack from the friends and relatives of the men killed Sunday. The greatest excitement prevails and women and children have been notified to keep off the streets. A mass meeting of the citizens was held today, and it was decided to send scouts out for two or three miles to give warning of the approach of the Leoti killers, when the citizens should form in line and fight guerilla fashion. It was

stated that more than 20 cowboys had been engaged by the Leoti people to form a part of the attacking force.

The report from Leoti is that the fighters are arming themselves with Winchesters and Colts, and say that they don't want to hurt anyone but the men who killed their friends, and they are going to have them if they have to kill everyone in Coronado. Three hundred dollars was spent in buying firearms, but no one knows when the attack will be made. Four men dead, three fatally injured and three seriously hurt represent the casualties so far.

A sign marking the site of Coronado still stands along the train tracks.

'Old' Ulysses

❖ Grant County ❖

Locals can credit the success of today's Ulysses to the debt of "old" Ulysses

C all it a tale of two cities - both with the same name. One boasts more than 6,100 people, along with a 4A high school. The other went broke and lies buried beneath the prairie grasses.

Ulysses, after all, was born twice - once in 1885 and a second time in 1909 when it escaped the banker.

The entire town loaded up and moved a few miles west.

A county seat battle

Settlement on the western Kansas plains was sparse when old Ulysses first sprouted, said Ginger Anthony, director of the Grant County Adobe Museum.

"Only a handful had settled in this part of the state," she said, adding there were a few open-ranged ranches that employed cowboys.

Grant County wouldn't even become a county for another three years, she said. But the tiny little town named after Gen. Ulysses S. Grant began to bustle with the Homestead Act, which gave settlers 160 acres of land to prove up.

George Earp, the first cousin of famous lawman Wyatt Earp, surveyed old Ulysses, Anthony said. Earp also was one of Ulysses' first promoters and the first mayor.

Population began to soar. A year after its inception, old Ulysses had more than 1,500 people living in it, according to the book "Ballots and Bullets: The Bloody County Seat Wars of Kansas" by Robert K. DeArment. The old town had several restaurants, a hotel, gambling houses and six saloons.

In 1888, Grant County was formed. Now all it needed was a county seat.

And, like many western Kansas counties during this same period, the battle began.

Residents in another new town, Appomattox, also wanted the county seat. The town had already gone through several name changes as tiny villages consolidated into one sizable community, according to DeArment.

Originally called Surprise, it had been named Tilden, then Cincinnati and eventually Appomattox, he wrote.

In February 1888, the Kansas Supreme Court gave Ulysses the county seat until an election could be held, DeArment reported.

A newspaper from a neighboring county remarked, "This is the old story over again ... surrender to Ulysses on the battlefield of Appomattox."

Several men from Dodge City were brought in to protect the ballot boxes.

There were never any shots fired because of the county seat election, but the county seat election of 1888 wouldn't be a clean one, Anthony said. Both towns employed "booglers" to move in for a time, which allowed them to vote on election day.

Ulysses founders began borrowing money from the east to pay potential voters. According to DeArment, one report was that Ulysses was offering $10 in cash for every vote and the number of "lawless characters" on the town's payroll reached nearly 300.

Meanwhile, according to DeArment, prosperous businessmen from Hutchinson were said to be providing the finances, including bribe money, to ensure Appomattox's victory.

However, an Appomattox bank employee recounted this story, which is in DeArment's book.

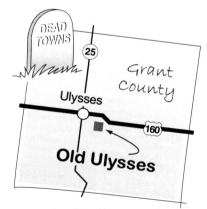

Location: About two miles east of present day Ulysses, south of U.S. 160.

The Hutchinson contingent that was to furnish the money to bribe enough voters to carry the election drove pompously up in front of the bank. One of the men got out for the benefit of the onlookers ... carried quite a large sack into the bank. I was the cashier at the time and was greeted cordially and presented with the sack that was full of apples. My heart sank, as I knew right then and there we were beaten for the county seat.

When it was all said and done, Ulysses had deeper pockets than Appomattox, thus winning the county seat election Oct. 16, 1888 by a 2,150-vote majority, DeArment wrote.

"Ulysses pretty much bought the county seat election," Anthony said, adding that despite illegal dealings as well, "Appomattox called foul."

The Kansas Supreme Court eventually ruled that another

'Old' Ulysses

election would take place. Votes again were cast in June 1890, which secured the county seat to Ulysses, Anthony said.

Meanwhile, many of the residents of Appomattox packed up and moved to Ulysses, according to DeArment's book.

Ulysses, however, would begin to struggle. Pioneers discovered the land wasn't great farm ground, especially without the advent of irrigation from the underground Ogallala Aquifer, which wouldn't occur prominently for at least another 50 years. Drought hit in the 1890s and caused population to wane. DeArment reported population went from 1,500 to eventually just 40.

Even Appomattox disappeared. By 1894, it lost its post office.

"A lot of these little towns, they were just a flash in the pan," Anthony said. "People came out here looking for free land, but if you can't make a living on free land, people leave."

"It was just a hard life," she said. "It was just one of those little prairie towns. It was struggling."

No money

Though Ulysses finally won the honor of county seat, the effort put it in debt, Anthony said. Leaders never paid interest on the bonds they received back in the late 1880s and the amount totaled more than $84,000.

Bonds came due in 1908, according to DeArment.

"There was no way they could pay that back," Anthony said. "And this little town already was on the brink of dying with 100 people here. They tried to pay the interest for one year and they decided it was impossible. Most of the people who had borrowed the money, they were shysters and had moved on. The people who stayed behind said it was like paying for a horse they didn't get to ride."

Even Earp had left in the early 1900s, she said. He moved to Wichita and became a U.S. deputy.

Leaders sent one of the residents to Kingman, where he purchased a quarter section of land that was located two miles to the west of old Ulysses.

"Then, they moved the old town site in 1909 and left the indebtedness behind. The hotel was split into three pieces in order to get it to the new location," Anthony said.

"It was an embarrassment to them to walk off and leave that debt, but they wanted a new start. They were cautious they didn't make those same mistakes again."

New Ulysses, as it was called, was located near the site of Appomattox. Another county seat election in June 1909 allowed the new city to move its courthouse and post office, Anthony said.

In 1921, residents dropped the "New" from the town's name, according to the Kansas State Historical Society. Population in 1920, according to the U.S. Census, was around 100.

A few memories

Robert Annis said he thinks his grandfather, Charlie Binney, was the county's register of deeds during the 1909 move, helping to haul the safe out of the courthouse. Meanwhile, his home was one of the last to be moved out of the old town.

His parents lived in the home when he was growing up, he said.

"My first memories were of living in that house," Annis said, adding that when his parents sold the property, the new owners tore down the house.

Binney came to Grant County to farm. He also hauled mail from old Ulysses to a few nearby towns. He later quit farming, bought the grocery store that had been moved out of old Ulysses and began working as a businessman.

His grandfather was a generous man, Annis said. Binney ran the store until he died in 1964. The family found $90,000 on the books of what people still owed him.

His grandmother would get a check on occasion from a customer who owed money.

"They'd write, 'If it hadn't been for Mr. Binney, we wouldn't have made it,' " Annis said. "He was just a good person - that he was."

In 1964, Binney's family razed the store and built a new structure, selling it to a clothing store. When the clothing store went bankrupt, the family took back the building.

The family still owns the building, which houses an art gallery and a clothing store, Annis said.

Little remains

Today, on the south side of U.S. 160 is what remains of old Ulysses, which is just a sea of grass now owned by the museum. All that is left is the concrete remains of the old school, as well as a metal silhouette put up by the museum a few years ago to mark the former town site.

The only building to survive the move still in Ulysses is the Hotel Edwards, said Anthony. The structure is part of the Grant County museum's facility.

Meanwhile, Ulysses High School is now in the location of where the former town of Appomattox sat.

"New" Ulysses celebrated its 100th birthday in 2009. If it was still kicking today, "old" Ulysses would have been 125 years old last year, Anthony said.

"If you look at a satellite picture, you can still see wagon roads," she said. "But there was so much blowing sand and dirt here in the 1930s, a lot of it is covered up."

Street scenes from Ulysses before it was moved from its original location on Feb. 6, 1909.

www.kansasmemory.org

Woodsdale

❖ Stevens County ❖

The fight between Hugoton and Woodsdale may have been the bloodiest county seat fight in the west

A lone Osage orange tree grows in the middle of a farm field on the barren western Kansas plains – the remaining remnant of a war between two towns and of cold-blooded murder.

The tree once was shade for Woodsdale's last building, a post office, but it closed in 1915. Local farmer Don Wilson, who owns the former town site near the intersection of roads 14 and V, said he once could see depressions of where basements had been located. These days, farm machinery has leveled much of the area.

On occasion, he said, he thinks about the old town while farming the land – its founder's dreams and the county seat war that ensued.

Other counties across Kansas had county seat wars, Wilson said.

"But not all had the bloodshed," he said.

A man and his dream

The Stevens County seat war is a story told by different individuals throughout the years, including The Hutchinson News. Some versions are slightly different. Overall, the story starts in 1885 with the birth of Hugoton.

Centrally located, settlers here wanted Hugoton to become the county seat and received a temporary declaration in 1886. However, Samuel Wood and I.C. Price started another town located about seven miles north of Hugoton. Wood aspired for the new town to overtake Hugoton and become the county seat, according to a paper written by Ken Butler on the website Blue Skyways – "Kansas Blood Spilled into Oklahoma."

Wood named his town Woodsdale, which in July 1886 included a blacksmith shop, an unfinished shanty, an unfinished office and a number of empty lots. Knowing he needed to help his town grow, Wood, a newspaper man with connections to papers in Council Grove and Cottonwood Falls, started a couple of newspapers and began to slander Hugoton, according to the book "Ballots and Bullets: The Bloody County Seat Wars of Kansas" by Robert K. DeArment.

DeArment wrote that Wood also aggrandized his town, hoping to attract more residents. He even went as far as to declare that parts of western Kansas and the future Oklahoma should become its own state, making Woodsdale the capital.

Some began to see through the talk.

One person wrote in the Hugo Herald in 1887, according to the book.

"…All the frauds in the way of towns I ever saw, Woodsdale, Stevens County, takes the cake. I was inveigled into believing it was the county seat of the county and paid it a visit, expecting to find a town in keeping with the beautiful country. Imagine my surprise when, on reaching it, I found it was composed in the main of holes in the ground and dry goods boxes for houses, not a single sign of paint or putty was visible…"

Wood realized he needed more than just good words to bolster Woodsdale. He offered free city lots to anyone who would build immediately.

By March 1, 1887, his town boasted 300 inhabitants, more than 75 homes and many business structures, according to the book. In addition, Wood hoped a railroad planned for Meade County would also go through Woodsdale. By attracting the railroad and new settlers, he would surely gain the county seat, according to a 1961 article in The News.

With the official county seat election approaching, Wood and Price started a trip to Topeka to protest the county's census, which would declare the county too little in population to be an official county. Under the law, a county had to have 2,500 people. The pair had conducted their own census, finding that the one done previously was fraudulent, listing several imaginary people who didn't live in the county.

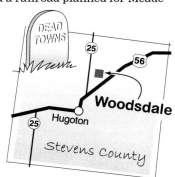

Location: About nine miles north of Hugoton, near the intersection of roads V and 14.

However, Hugoton men surrounded Price and Wood early in the journey, taking them into custody. Butler's article says the two were placed on trial, found guilty and were sentenced to go with a buffalo hunting party to "No Man's Land" – an area that is now the Oklahoma panhandle. However, there hadn't been buffalo in the area for years.

Wood, hearing his captors argue about he and Price's fate, left a note to his wife of what was happening, hoping someone

Woodsdale

would stumble upon it, according to the book.

They did. A Woodsdale group, already suspicious, found the note at the abandoned campsite. They eventually caught up with Wood and his captors, and Wood later filed civil and criminal proceedings against the Hugoton folks. However a judge dismissed charges due to lack of evidence, according to the book. The state named Hugoton the permanent county seat in 1887.

Bad feelings continue

A man named Sam Robinson built a hotel in Woodsdale, taking advantage of the free lots. But when Wood didn't support his bid for the county sheriff, he moved the hotel to Hugoton. Robinson eventually lost the sheriff's race to Wood's choice, John Cross. Yet, his hatred for Wood and Woodsdale gave him popularity in Hugoton, which landed him the job as the Hugoton marshal, according to The News.

Meanwhile, Cross kept his office in Woodsdale, despite the fact Hugoton was the county seat. Wood continued trying to promote a town, as well as a railroad – still hopeful that a train through Woodsdale would gain him the county seat. Hugoton's founders had him arrested for libel, with Wood quickly posting bond in time to put out another edition of his newspaper.

More sparks flew in spring 1888 during a meeting at the now ghost town of Voorhees regarding the railroad bonds.

Deputy Sheriff J.G. Gerrond, who was speaking for Wood (who could not be present), was "knocked senseless by a blow from the pistol" of Robinson. This brought about a fight, according to an article in The News. A warrant was issued for Robinson's arrest, but when Woodsdale Marshal Ed Short went to Hugoton to arrest Robinson, a gunfight erupted between the two men, with the men of Hugoton running Short out of town.

In late June, a railroad bond election was held, but not without controversy. Sheriff Cross called in the state militia, which made it clear that the vote counting wasn't going to happen without conflict. General Murrey Myers and his unit went to the area and disarmed forces in both towns, according to DeArment's book.

Climax

Still trying to serve a warrant on Robinson, Short learned in July 1888 that Robinson, with his family and some friends, had gone into the "Neutral Strip" across the border in Oklahoma to camp, fish and pick wild plums. Short and his posse located Robinson, who was not with the others. Short sent word back to Woodsdale that he needed more men.

Robinson, soon aware of Short's approaching posse, decided to head to Hugoton to avoid a gunfight around women and children. Meanwhile, Sheriff Cross received Short's message. He recruited Ted Eaton, Bob Hubbard, Roland Wilcox and Herbert Tonney to head with him to the border.

When the sheriff and his men reached the camp, Cross found out that Short had departed, leaving notice for Cross to return to Woodsdale, according to DeArment's book. As Robinson neared Hugoton, he met a band of Hugoton men who had started south to locate and help their city marshal. The group chased Short and his posse back into Woodsdale. Aware that Cross left Woodsdale, Robinson and his men decided to locate Cross and his men while they were outside Stevens County.

On July 25, 1888, Cross' group came upon the Haas family, who were haying on land close to a place known as the Wild Horse Lake, which is about eight miles south of the Kansas border, DeArment wrote. They decided to camp there for the night.

Not long after the Woodsdale men had gone to sleep, the

Samuel Newitt Wood was an active participant on behalf of the free state cause. He served in the Kansas Territory Legislature and was a delegate to the Leavenworth Constitutional Convention. He was also involved in some of the armed conflicts during the territorial era. He eventually founded the Stevens County town of Woodsdale.

www.kansasmemory.org

Hugoton men came upon the hay meadow camp, according to a 1920 article in The News. All weapons were taken from the sheriff and his men. One by one, Robinson and his men shot each man. He also shot a few of the men twice to make sure they were dead – all except for Tonney, a 16- or 17-year-old boy they thought was definitely dead.

The group left, telling the Haas family to follow them back to Hugoton. Confident all had left, Tonney made his way to his horse and eventually back into Kansas to Voorhees, where he received medical treatment.

The battle had reached its climax with the state militia again coming to the county. Robinson, however, already had fled town.

Justice never came. With the exception of Robinson, who had been arrested in Colorado and sentenced to 14 years in Colorado State Penitentiary for robbing a store, the men who were part of the killings were found guilty and sentenced to hanging, according to a Fort Hays State University article. The verdict, however, was appealed to the U.S. Supreme Court, and in January 1891, the court ruled the convictions voided because the area the murders took place weren't under a court jurisdiction.

The end was nearing for Woodsdale, and for Wood, as well. When Wood went to Hugoton on June 23, 1891 to answer a bribery charge, James Brennan shot him in the back as he entered the courthouse. Wood tried to escape, but he was shot two more times.

The judicial system didn't charge Brennan, either. According to the Fort Hays article, he got off for several reasons, including the fact it had been determined he could not receive a fair trial in Stevens County and a change of venue was never requested, because under Kansas law at that time, only the defense could request it. There also was another law that stated if an accused man was being held without bond and had not been tried in two regular court sessions, he was to be released.

One other incident occurred over the years. Bonnie Parker and Clyde Barrow, the infamous Bonnie and Clyde, lived near the old site of Woodsdale and assumed other names, according to story in The News from 1969. Claude French told a News reporter the two went by the names of Jewell and Blackie, and "Jewell" had a café in Hugoton while Blackie worked for a local farmer.

They left town quickly after a man named Fred McBee, whom French thinks was slipped something into his drink at the café to make him inebriated, started causing problems in town and Sheriff Charlie Newman tried to arrest him. McBee grabbed the sheriff's gun and shot him dead.

Only stories

Gladys Renfro, curator at the Stevens County Gas and Historical Museum, said all that remains these days of Woodsdale are just stories. Even the old grudges among residents

Woodsdale

The large school at Woodsdale was offered for public sale in April 1902 and then torn down.

Stevens County Gas and Historical Museum

have been long gone.

Wilson said there are a few locals related to those in the story, noting most names have changed through marriage.

Teresa Harder's great-grandfather was James Copeland Gerrond, the deputy sheriff hit with the pistol by Robinson during the railroad meeting. She said Gerrond took one of the men back to Missouri for burial.

She said she has explored the area and found the old family dugout near Woodsdale.

Wilson said he used to find old inkwells and dolls at the location of the school. He also has found bullets around where the old tavern – or "drug store" – once sat. Serving liquor, of course, was against the law, except for medicinal purposes.

"The cowboys would empty their pistols in the air before they went into the saloon," Wilson said. "We used to have quite a collection."

Wilson, whose parents bought the property in 1924, said they discovered the Woodsdale well sometime in the 1930s. His father's hired hand went out to grade roads and came back to the farm saying there was a deep hole out there. They filled in the well.

The Stevens County history book talks about the passing of Woodsdale when the school was razed in 1902.

"All that remains are the memories which cling to the name of Woodsdale – the dreams and hopes of its people, the hours and days of despair faced by the people of Woodsdale. Memories, which bring back the time when a majority of the citizens of this county were armed to the teeth, ready at the word to defend their town and their homes. "…May the memories of Woodsdale be only pleasant ones, and the ghosts of a ghost town remain silent."

The Story of an Outlaw

This is the personal account of Herbert M. Tonney, who survived the Hay Meadow Massacre. His tale is told in the book "The Story of an Outlaw" by Emerson Hough in 1907.

The first I heard was Cross exclaiming, "They have got us!" At that time there was shooting, and Robinson called out, "Boys, close in!" He called out to Cross, "Surrender, and hold up your hands!" Our arms were mostly against the haystacks. Not one of us fired a shot, or could have done so at that moment.

Sheriff Cross, Hubbard, and myself got up and stood together. We held up our hands. They did not seem to notice Wilcox and Eaton, who were lying in the wagon. ...

Robinson exclaimed, "Sheriff Cross, you are my first man."

He raised his Winchester and fired at Cross, a distance of a few feet, and I saw Cross fall dead at my side. It was all a sort of trance or dream to me. I did not seem to realize what was going on, but knew that I could make no resistance. My gun was not within reach. I knew that I, too, would be shot down.

Hubbard had now been disarmed, if indeed he had on any weapon. Robinson remarked to him, "I want you, too!" and as he spoke he raised his Winchester and shot him dead, Hubbard also falling close to where I stood, his murderer being but a few feet from him.

I knew that my turn must come pretty soon. It was Chamberlain who was to be my executioner, J. B. Chamberlain, chairman of the board of county commissioners of Stevens County and always prominent in Hugoton matters. Chamber-

21

Woodsdale

lain was about eight feet from me, or perhaps less, when he raised his rifle deliberately to kill me. There were powder burns on my neck and face from the shot, as the woman who cared for me on the following day testified in court.

I saw the rifle leveled, and realized that I was going to be killed. Instinctively, I flinched to one side of the line of the rifle. That saved my life. The ball entered the left side of my neck, about three-quarters of an inch from the carotid artery and about half an inch above the left clavicle, coming out through the left shoulder. I felt no pain at the time, and, indeed, did not feel pain until the next day. The shock of the shot knocked me down and numbed me, and I suppose I lay a minute or two before I recovered sensation or knew anything about my condition. It was supposed by all that I was killed, and, in a vague way, I agreed that I must be killed; that my spirit was simply present listening and seeing.

Eaton had now got out of the wagon, and he started to run towards the horses. Robinson and one or two others now turned and pursued him, and I heard a shot or so.

... Then I heard the Hugoton men talking and declaring that they must have the fifth man of our party, whom they had not yet found. At this time, old man Haas and his sons came and stood near where I was and saw me looking up. The former, seeing that I was not dead, asked me where I had been shot.

... At this moment I heard the Hugoton men starting toward me, and I dropped back and feigned death. Haas did not betray me. The Hugoton men now lit matches and peered into the faces of their victims to see if they were dead. I kept my eyes shut when the matches were held to my face and held my breath.

They finally found Wilcox, I do not know just where, but they stood him up within fifteen feet of where I was lying feigning death. They asked Wilcox what he had been doing there, and he replied that he had just been down on the Strip looking around.

"That's a damned lie!" replied Robinson, the head executioner. As he spoke, he raised his Winchester and fired. Wilcox fell, and as he lay he moaned a little bit, as I heard, "Put the fellow out of his misery," ... Someone then apparently fired a revolver shot and Wilcox became silent.

Someone came to me, took hold of my foot, and began to pull me around to see whether I was dead. Robinson wanted it made sure. Chamberlain, my executioner, said, "He's dead; I gave him a center shot. I don't need to shoot a man twice at that distance."

Either Chamberlain or some one else took me by the legs, dragged me about, and kicked me in the side, leaving bruises which were visible for many days afterwards. I feigned death so well that they did not shoot me again. They did shoot a second time each of the others who lay near me. We found seven cartridges on the ground near where the killing was done.

... After the party had been gone about twenty minutes, I found I could get on my feet, although I was very weak. At first, I went and examined Wilcox, Cross and Hubbard and found they were quite dead. Their belts and guns were gone. Then I went to get my horse. It was hard for me to get into the saddle, and it has always seemed to me providential that I could do so at all. My horse was very wild and difficult to mount under ordinary circumstances. Now, it seemed to me that he knew my plight. It is certain that at that time and afterwards he was perfectly quiet and gentle, even when I laboriously tried to get into the saddle.

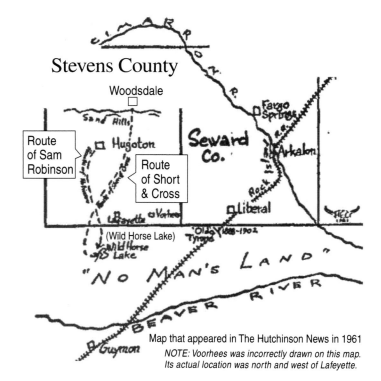

Map that appeared in The Hutchinson News in 1961

NOTE: Voorhees was incorrectly drawn on this map. Its actual location was north and west of Lafeyette.

The Hay Meadow Massacre took place in a hay meadow across the border in Oklahoma. Sam Robinson, Hugoton, and his posse of men, shot one by one a group from Woodsdale that included Stevens County Sheriff John Cross. They shot most of the men twice to make sure they were dead – all except Herbert Tonney, who was able to ride into Kansas after the group had left the scene. This photograph was sent to the Wichita Eagle in 1911. The photographer who sent it had reached the scene of the murders the morning after the shootings. The victims still lay where they had fallen.

Ravanna

❖ Finney County ❖

Former county seat of defunct Garfield County is just a pile of stone ruins

Driving his pickup on a dirt road sandwiched between two limestone ruins, 86-year-old Guy Reed noted there could be a rattler or two out during the first warm days of March.

In the summers, at least, an infestation of rattlesnakes is about all that makes up this area of Finney County once populated by more than 700 residents. Even a few sons of P.T. Barnum's famed Siamese twins, Eng and Chang, once lived in this dead town, said Reed, adding matter-of-factly that he didn't know how they fathered nearly two dozen children.

Ravanna's story, however, is deeper than rattlesnakes and the children of conjoined brothers. It is about the bitter battle with nearby neighbor Eminence for the county seat of a now nonexistent county. Reed recalled attending his first year of school at Ravanna in 1930. Today, however, just an outline of a school remains – the walls already crumbled to the ground from age and weather.

"I hate to see the building torn down," he said.

Misnamed

Born during the first 40 years of the state's history, Garfield County formed as residents moved westward, many taking advantage of the government's Homestead Act. It was comprised of a territory once called Buffalo County, although this county, which was made up of areas of present-day Finney and Lane counties, never was officially organized, according to the Kansas State Historical Society.

At this time, Buffalo Center was the first town that residents tried to establish as a county seat, as it was in the center of the county. However, the area didn't have good water, said Laurie Oshel, assistant director of the Finney County Historical Museum.

Thus, they set their eyes on what soon would be Ravanna, she said. Originally, it was called Mason, established in 1879, and Samuel Wood was the first postmaster. A year later, the town became Cowland, after the first settler, John Bull. Some also unofficially called it Bulltown, but both names didn't receive a liking from locals.

They adopted Ravanna in September 1885, after a resident, James Cross, suggested naming it after his native Ravenna, Ohio.

"They misspelled it," Oshel said with a laugh.

Ravanna had a cheese plant, merchants, a livery, black-

smith, two dentists and a doctor, among other entrepreneurs. One of the Siamese twins' sons, Fred, was a druggist. Guy Reed's grandparents had a creamery. There also was a church, hotel, bank and school. And work soon started on what Ravanna planned would be the Garfield County Courthouse, which cost $10,000.

Flyers were printed and ads ran in area newspapers promoting the town.

RAVANNA! The Future County Seat of Garfield Co. A Real Town Backed by Unlimited Wealth! A Future City! The Place to Invest!

However, not far west, another town was emerging, she said. Established with the help of C.J. "Buffalo" Jones, it was first called Cuyler before they settled on Creola.

"But when the name was sent in for the town, they found out there already was a town in Kansas by that name," Oshel said. "So it was changed to Eminence in 1887."

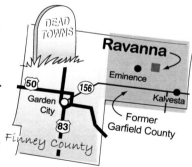

Location: Four miles east of Highway 23 at the intersection of Lake and Ravanna roads in Finney County.

County seat battles

Folks in Eminence wanted the county seat just as badly as Ravanna. It's even said that in 1887, Buffalo Jones hired Bat Masterson and 20 lawmen from Dodge City to help keep the peace, according to the Kansas State Historical Society. However, Oshel said, others have said Masterson was not in the area during this time.

"It's entirely possible he was there if he was in the area," she said, "but it's hard to prove anything."

Later that year, residents cast their ballots, declaring Ravanna the county seat by 35 votes. Eminence protested, saying that Ravanna residents stuffed the ballot box.

"They had a lawsuit and the (Kansas) Supreme Court

Ravanna

Today, just an outline of a school remains at the ghost town of Ravanna. The walls have crumbled to the ground from age and weather. The town died after its bitter battle with nearby neighbor Eminence for the county seat of now nonexistent Garfield County. The school closed in the 1930s.

Amy Bickel/The Hutchinson News

proved the ballot boxes were stuffed and the decision went to Eminence," Oshel said.

That was in 1889, she said, noting that the Ravanna courthouse was just being completed when the reversal took place.

A New York Times article for that year said the state militia was called in to stop conflicts, which included Eminence trying to take the county records from Ravanna. In one attempt, Eminence residents tried to remove the treasurer's office and its safe, which Ravanna residents were able to secure, although the safe was badly damaged, according to an article in The Hutchinson News.

Ravanna continued to try to hold on to the seat, despite a court order to turn over the county records. However, Eminence citizens raided Ravanna at night, broke into the courthouse and swiped the records.

Then, in 1891, according to The Times, the state's adjutant general headed to Ravanna after getting word that both towns were claiming to be the county seat with Ravanna organizing an armed force to take the records now stored at Eminence.

Arguments continued on both sides, with Ravanna residents deciding that if they couldn't win, no one would, Oshel said. According to a 1985 newspaper story, a Ravanna faction began a letter-writing campaign that got the attention of Kansas Attorney General John Ives. In late 1892, he and the Garfield County Commission agreed that if an impartial survey showed the county to have less than 432 square miles, the required amount under statute needed, the county would be dissolved.

"It had less than 432 square miles," Oshel said, noting it was just a few miles short of being considered a true county. "It was illegally organized."

Garfield County was annexed to Finney County in 1893, she said. Meanwhile, a period of good crops soon dried up. With times tough, the area began to disperse.

Dead town, dead county

As evening approached the area of the county where he farmed and ranched, Guy Reed walked around the old Ravanna Cemetery. His aunt is buried here, he said, but with the graves worn and grass-covered, he couldn't pinpoint the location.

Not quite a half-mile away are the ruins, which stick up like pillars on the barren prairie. They are the stone remains of the school Reed attended and the old courthouse, which never was used, he said. A fire struck the courthouse around the turn of the century – leaving just the outer stone shell.

Mike O'Brate, who farms and ranches in the area and owns the old school site, said folks with metal detectors have found coins, but most relics have been stripped clean from the location. For instance, 30 or 40 years ago the courthouse jail's bars still stood in a window – until one day someone stole them.

Reed said the school closed in the late 1930s. It was a two-story structure built for the masses, but the grades only needed to use one room on the main floor.

Around the time the school closed, a Works Progress Administration project began taking rock from the area to build Dighton High School's football field stands and a stonewall surrounding the track, said former Dighton School Superintendent Angela Lawrence. A grant a few years ago helped repair the aging structure.

Except for the cemetery a half-mile away, nothing else remains of Ravanna, Reed said.

There's talk that a railroad was heading to Ravanna until the company ran out of money, he said, adding, "if that railroad would have come through, it might have made the difference."

Now population in the former county is few, Reed said. Nearby Kalvesta, another ghost town to the south, has a few houses, an elevator and a dealership, but that's about it, he said.

"It makes it rough. People get better jobs and move away," he said.

Ravanna

From The Hutchinson News, Sept. 13, 1889.

Bad Blood Between Ravanna and Eminence, in Garfield County.

TOPEKA, Kan., Sept. 13 – The bitter feeling between the citizens of Ravanna and Eminence over the unsettled county seat question was renewed yesterday by the removal by W. T. Williams, treasurer of the county, of the records of his office, from Ravenna to Eminence. A guard of Ravanna citizens had been detailed to watch the treasurer to prevent the removal.

Yesterday the guards attended the judicial district convention. Williams loaded the records of his office into a wagon and was about to drive off when the alarm was given. The guards hurried from the convention and arming themselves and hastily hitching up a team, started in pursuit of the fleeing treasurer. At a crossroad, they mistook another wagon for the treasurer's and followed the wrong trail. They were too slow for the team in advance and in their rage fired several shots at the supposed fugitive, who finally escaped.

In the meantime, Williams had reached Eminence and put the records in place of security.

The citizens of Eminence have armed themselves in anticipation of an attempt by the Ravanna people to capture the records and return them to their city.

Guy Reed, 86, walks through the old Ravanna Cemetery near the site of the former county seat of the new nonexistent Garfield County. Reed's aunt is buried in the cemetery, although he isn't sure where.

Some of the stones in the Ravanna Cemetery are hard to read or are covered in grass.

Photos by Amy Bickel/The Hutchinson News

Ruins of the Garfield County Courthouse still stand in a pasture in Ravanna. The courthouse was never used, as Garfield was declared an illegal county. The structure burned at the turn of the 20th century.

Amy

❖ Lane County ❖

*The razing of the Amy Baptist Church leaves only a few structures left –
a few homes, a large grain elevator and a dilapidated school*

The pews are long gone and the sound of singing voices hasn't been heard here in a good 30 years.

Not that there aren't signs of a past life at the weather-beaten Amy Baptist Church, which, still stood on this November day in 2010.

A torn green curtain hung by the pulpit. Dusty books and hymnals lined a few shelves in the basement, some more than a century old. An old attendance record sheet was part of the litter on the floor, along with a few Christmas decorations.

And a sign quoting a Bible verse from the Gospel of John, which was situated above the basement's kitchen, read:

"Jesus said, 'I am the resurrection, and the life: he who believeth in me shall live and not die.' "

Garden City Co-op branch manager Ryan Herman and employee Bentz Lewis walked through the church on a warm fall afternoon, air filtering through the windows and litter crunching at their feet. Lewis peered up into the old steeple, where, it seemed, an owl or another bird had found a home.

"It's seen better days," said Lewis, who rummaged through some of the books in the basement, finding one that dated back to 1897.

However, said Amy's branch manager Herman at the time, within a few days, the church would see its ultimate demise.

By Thanksgiving, the little house of worship was no longer – the cooperative demolished the dilapidated structure.

These days, the mammoth grain elevator, an abandoned elementary school and a couple of homes is all that is left of Amy – a town once a small center of activity on the High Plains of Kansas.

The town located just west of Dighton on Kansas Highway 96 once had a lumberyard and a general store. The town even had a band – complete with uniforms – and a bandstand.

Location: About seven miles west of Dighton on Highway 96.

"It had activity," said Pat Herndon, who owns The Old Bank Gallery in the nearby county seat town of Dighton. "But it never had a big population."

Amy started back in the late 1800s as Ellen – a stop established by the railroad, said Joel Herndon, Pat's son, who also serves on the Lane County Historical Society board.

However, it wasn't until 1906 that the town began to thrive, and the town was renamed Amy, Pat Herndon said. Nolan Yates, who started the post office that year, applied for a permit with the U.S. Postal Service, but his request was denied because Ellen was already a name of another town in eastern Kansas.

Not knowing what to name his community, Yates picked names of local teenaged girls and submitted them to the postal service. An official there picked Amy, after 16-year-old Amy Bruner.

Herndon said her husband's grandfather, John Herndon, started the lumberyard around that same time the town changed its name. A grocery also opened in 1906, according to an old advertisement sign salvaged from the store that now hangs in an area farmer Vance Ehmke's work shed.

It was during this time the town prospered, Pat Herndon said. With nothing more than a horse-drawn buggy to get families from place to place, residents often traveled to the nearest town for social gatherings, such as playing baseball or attending a concert. There were children's games and even a small merry-go-round with an organ music box – the riders pumping the ride to move – similar to an old-style railroad handcar.

Those are just a few of the stories that former residents have passed down generation to generation, Herndon said. She herself moved to Amy in 1961 after marrying her husband, Walter. The couple lived there until 2002, when they moved into Dighton. It is also where they attended church for a number of years, she and her husband serving as youth sponsors in the 1960s.

Joel Herndon said he even played baby Jesus for one of the Christmas programs.

"That was when I was really little, of course," he said with a chuckle.

The Herndon family was among the first church members and the last, Herndon said. Her father-law-in, William Walter Herndon, was a regular parishioner until the church closed in the 1970s.

Amy

For years, the church stood in the shadows of the elevator, which still bustles with farmers, especially during the harvest seasons. Across the highway is the old Amy School District No. 4 building. The old play equipment are nearly hidden by weeds.

The school closed around 1980, Pat Herndon said, noting son Joel attended the school until the fourth grade. It served as a voting spot for a while before the Kansas climate took its toll.

Other buildings are long gone. The post office closed in 1954.

The store was torn down in the mid-2000s. Any traces of the lumberyard and bandstand have disappeared, as well.

And, on a fall day in 2010, the church met the same fate. It, along with a home nearby, was razed by the cooperative – making way for progress.

One of the last remnants of Amy's early history – once the focal point of this little community – vanished for good.

"It always hurts to see a piece of history go," Pat Herndon said. "But it's in such terrible shape. I'd rather see it go like that than to have it collapse on its own."

Photos by Lindsey Bauman/The Hutchinson News

The old Amy Baptist Church and an empty house prior to being torn down, shown in front of the Amy branch of the Garden City Coop.

An attendance chart was in the basement of the Amy Baptist Church before it was demolished.

Alamota

❖ Lane County ❖

After the Great Depression, Alamota was never quite the same

As an early 1900s postcard showing young lovers hugging states, "I could stay in Alamota forever and ever."

Yet, on this fall day, a walk along the deserted main street is eerily quiet, except for the Kansas wind and a sprinkler running in the yard of one of the community's three remaining homes. The only human activity on this morning was a postal worker who stopped to deliver mail and a couple of drivers in farm trucks, which kicked up dust as they drove by.

Meanwhile, the lasting business, a grain elevator, had already closed for the season.

Most who used to frequent this little town back in its heyday have packed up and moved away.

"I'm the one holding down the fort now, and I don't know why," said 76- year-old Joanie Trebilcock with a laugh – who grew up in the town her grandparents helped establish.

She is one of at least four people who still call Alamota home – the Lane County town that once had a hotel, a store, a restaurant, school, fuel stop and lumberyard, along with a bank her father, Winslow, ran.

Nevertheless, these days, the town once vibrant with activity is abandoned and crumbling. The roof of the family bank has fallen in and the old restaurant and store are only shells.

Except for the towering grain elevator that peeks above the terrain, the Lane County ghost town is hidden from the sight of those traveling along nearby Kansas Highway 96 – a passing thought, if that, as folks head east or west. Except, that is, for a few like Trebilcock.

"I'm very sentimental about that town," she said.

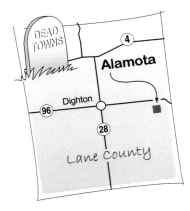

Location: One mile south of Highway 96 near the intersection of 380 Road.

"Like living on a farm"

Alamota, about 10 miles east of the county seat town of Dighton, started in 1877 along present-day K-96 as a post office, according to the Kansas State Historical Society.

The town even had a brick factory. However, when the railroad was built about a mile or so south of the former town site, residents decided to move Alamota to be closer to what they considered a lifeline, Trebilcock said she suspects.

The post office closed in the previous Alamota in 1894 and reopened in 1903, according to the historical society.

It was in 1902 that two men – farmer William Durr and businessman Richard Church – convinced their friend from Holyrood, Trebilcock's grandfather, Frank Vycital Sr., to come and help build a commerce center, said Ellen May Stanley, who lived on a farm near Alamota and has written several books on Lane County's history.

Vycital moved his family, including sons Frank Jr. and Winslow, who was just a toddler, Stanley said. They opened a store, followed by the hotel. According to a historical document, the town had at least 40 people in the nearby vicinity by 1910.

In 1923, after Winslow graduated from college and married, he came home and started the bank, as well as operated an insurance business, Trebilcock said. When the Great Depression hit in the 1930s, her father's bank closed, never reopening after President Franklin Roosevelt's "bank holiday."

Yet her father stayed busy selling insurance until he died in 1972, making enough to put both her and her brother through college.

After the Depression, the town never was as big as when it first started, she said, but added there was plenty of activity.

"It was like living on a farm, but you weren't," she said. "We had a horse, we went to school."

Trebilcock attended the elementary school through the eighth grade, then went to Dighton High School. And like many in rural settings, she went on to college in a big city – Colorado Springs –where she eventually married and raised her family instead of coming back to rural Lane County.

However, every Christmas, as well as other times of the year, she, her husband and her children would make the four-hour trip back to Alamota to celebrate the season with family.

Over the years, the town began to dwindle even more. The hotel shut down in the 1940s. Her uncle's store and post office burned down in the 1950s. He reopened it in the hotel, but on a

Alamota

much smaller scale before closing not many years later.

The school closed in the 1970s, and it is now used by a local farmer as a machine shop. The post office, still visible through the windows of the old hotel, closed in 1992.

Still a place they call home

Don and May Thomas have lived in town for more than 60 years – first in the rooms of the old hotel before moving after the mercantile fire to a small house across the railroad tracks.

Don Thomas said he grew up on a nearby farm, coming to town with his family for supplies. He recalled the town having three elevators, including a Garvey elevator.

A lot has changed, he said, pointing to a photocopied picture of Alamota's downtown area.

It's sad to see the town dwindle away, he said.

Trebilcock said she and her husband returned to Alamota in the 1990s to care for her mother, who passed away at age 100 in 2002. Now she frequents two towns, both Alamota and Great Bend, where a daughter and grandchildren live.

However, she said, she has passed down the love of her hometown to her children, noting she tells them fondly of her memories. Family gatherings by the grandchildren are requested to take place at "the farm."

"It was a great place to ride your bike – no crime and lots of chickens," she said. "It was a great place to grow up."

Photos by Lindsey Bauman/The Hutchinson News

The old hotel in Alamota still stands, with the post office visible inside. Next door is the bank, which closed in the 1930s.

The Alamota school closed in the 1970s and is currently being used as a machine shop.

Buda

❖ Ness County ❖

The town wasn't much, but it was a community center for the population around it.

There was not much in this little spot when Earl McVicker's ancestors first homesteaded here, a family with three children at the time, all living in a small dugout on a parcel of untouched prairie.

Buda, however, didn't have to be big to be a gathering place for area farmers and others – a place where residents met for potlucks and songs. The town of sorts did once have a hotel, a grocery and a post office in the 1800s and, of course, founders had dreams of it getting bigger. Yet, it never did and that didn't seem to matter to the locals around it.

Buda is where McVicker and his siblings received their education, which was in a one-room brick structure that housed children from first to eighth grade. There also was a Sunday school, potluck dinners, pie auctions and other events that each week drew residents from a radius around Buda.

These days, McVicker says, only the memories are left of the area where he grew up. Farmers who once supported the community have died. The school/church was torn down more than a decade ago. All that is left is a cemetery where McVicker's parents, Dean and Harriet, as well as his ancestors, are buried – a place he visits several times a year.

He reminisced about his youth there in the 1950s and 60s – a place, he says, that impacted him and his siblings.

"It was a very close and friendly community," said McVicker, who went on to college and now is a president of Central Bank and Trust in Hutchinson. "Even if we weren't related, we worked and support each other."

Good memories

Founders had visions for this little town. A post office existed as early as 1879 in what was then called Newby, according to the Kansas State Historical Society.

And in 1880, the original town of Buda was platted and laid out with an ox team pulling a walking plow, according to the records of Edwin Goodman, a member of one of the homesteading families of the area.

In 1882, according to the historical society, the name of the post office was changed to Buda, although no one knows exactly why or how anyone came up with the name, said McVicker's sister, Cheryl Lewis, of Wichita, who wrote a couple books about the family history in the area with her sister, Linda Fields, of Texas.

"People think it's pronounced Boo-da, but it's always been Beu-da," she said.

No matter the name, dreams of a flourishing village were short-lived. While there was the hotel of sorts and a grocery, the railroad went through 12 miles to the north, and Buda, it seemed, would be nothing more than a rural community gathering place, said Helen Hanks, who grew up on a farm not far from the community.

"It was just a paper town," Hanks said. "When they found out the railroad wasn't going through," they abandoned the idea.

Besides the failing town, life on the prairie wasn't easy. Hanks recorded a few notes about Buda, taken from the documents and diaries of others.

That includes deaths. For instance, in 1887, a 19 year-old wife died after she fought a prairie fire to the point of exhaustion. In 1913, a 7-year-old girl died after being struck by a rattlesnake. Meanwhile, the first death at Buda Cemetery was in 1883 when a 12-year old boy attempted to brave a blizzard to find his pet dog.

Life continued, however, Hanks said. A school built in the early 1880s was replaced in 1921. A Sunday school that had closed in the 1890s was reorganized in the 1920s as well.

Besides Sunday school at the school building, Hanks recalls attending literary events. In the schoolyard, there were ball games and bronc riding exhibitions.

Even after the school closed for good in the 1960s, residents still gathered at Buda for the weekly Sunday school and other activities, Lewis said. She recalls making a pie for the boxed-pie auction. The highest bidder of a pie would eat it with the baker.

Pie auctions around Halloween helped fund Christmas activities, Hanks said.

Location:
About 12 miles south of Beeler in southwest Ness County.

Buda

"Everything happened at little Buda," Hanks said. "For some reason, it hung on as a community for a long, long time.

"Now all that is left are the people and the memories," she said. "And I have no bad memories."

Little left

Hanks noted that for years former resident Goodman could see the streets that once had been platted. However, the days of the dust storms covered much of what remained.

Now all that is left of Buda is the Buda Cemetery where a marble marker depicts the spot of the first Buda School. Just down the road to the west is a concrete slab – all that remains of the second school.

The history, however, lives on through former residents, says Lewis.

"It's a love my dad and I shared of the Buda community," she said of Dean McVicker. "I loved hearing him tell the stories. He knew a lot of the history."

That may be because the family roots are so deep. Lewis and McVicker's great-grandparents, George and Mary Slagle, first

came to the area in the mid-1880s, living in the dugout for a few years with three of their children. Eventually, they built a stone house where they raised seven children in all.

The stone house is in disrepair but still stands and is owned by their brother, Daryl McVicker.

Their grandmother, Annie Slagle, actually perfected a homestead herself before she married her grandfather, Ernest McVicker. Annie's homestead still is in the family.

Meanwhile, their relatives taught at the school and their grandfather, Lloyd Webb, also was the Sunday school superintendent.

"I just have a love for the local history," Lewis said. "I have so much family that first settled there."

Hanks said when the owner tore down the brick school at the turn of the 21st century, he said anyone who wanted the bricks could come and get them. She and her husband, Joe, used the bricks when constructing their new home.

"We hauled in bricks and laid them in our foyer," she said, noting they sometimes joke to visitors that "you are standing on hallowed ground."

Photos courtesy Helen Hanks

A windmill stands near the site of the Buda cemetery in Ness County.

The first Buda School was built in the 1880's at the site of the Buda Cemetery and closed in 1921. A new school was then constructed. Children first through eighth grade attended school in the one-room school structure until the 1960's.

Harold

❖ Ness County ❖

Little town in Ness County is now a hunting lodge

The railroad, they said, was sure to come to this fledgling town amid a fertile valley.

The growing town of Harold, after all, already had a hotel, jewelry store and newspaper. There also was a post office, a general store and a school. It had everything, it seems, that a new town on the prairie needed – except for a railroad.

"The Rock Island is fast covering all the good territory not already occupied; the B&M of Nebraska wants to come this way and Frisco is rapidly pushing west and wants the best line possible," according to the author of Handbook of Ness County, Kansas 1887. "The Fort Smith is looking in the same direction and Harold will get one or two of these lines and then she will boom; she cannot help it."

The boom, however, never came. Those trains went elsewhere and so did the Denver, Memphis and Atlantic, the town's last hope for a rail.

"It faded away when the railroad did not go through," said Bill Miner, whose great-grandfather, William D. Miner, whom he is named for, was the founder and president of the Harold Town Co. The railroad, instead, went north to Ransom, and little Harold virtually disappeared, Bill Miner said.

A goal of prosperity

William Miner and W.N. Dilley of Harold founded Harold in May 1886. It was 12 miles south and two miles west of Ness City, just west of present-day Highway 283.

When looking over the site with Dilley, his great-grandfather had brought his 4- year-old son, Harold, Bill Miner said. Thus, the town became Harold.

William Miner, a Ness City real estate businessman, was a town promoter, as well. He had interest in Ransom, to the

Location: About 12 miles south and two miles west of Ness City, just west of present-day Highway 283.

north, and had hopes for Harold to prosper.

Harold started like no other ghost city. Instead of sod buildings, much of the town's infrastructure was made of stone or frame, according to the handbook. It also had potential, according to the writer of the 1887 handbook.

"The town has a faultless location on a pretty plateau overlooking the river and valley, is surrounded by one of the fairest and most fertile valley regions in Kansas and, like Bazine, has an admirable water supply, living wells being easily and cheaply obtained at a depth of 25 and 30 feet. Here, too, as at Bazine and Ness City, there is no end of superb white and cream-colored building stones and fine building sand. What was a wild prairie in the midst of Mr. W.N. Dilley's farm little more than a year ago, is now the scene of busy village life, the evidences of which are the handsome stone Town Co. building and town hall; the pretty new M.E. Church, half a dozen business buildings, a large stone livery barn, the stone post office, Record building, the Harold House, a feed mill, several shops and a group of pretty cottage homes.

At one time, Harold boasted having the best baseball team in the area. There also was a creamery just down the section.

In 1887, the township peaked at as many as 862 people, according to Minnie Millbrook's book "Ness, Western County, Kansas," published in 1955.

Harold had a few needs, the author of the handbook wrote. There wasn't a skilled blacksmith or a tinner. There also wasn't a harness and saddle shop, nor was there a hardware store. The biggest thing Harold was missing, the author reported, was the railway.

Still, according to the handbook,

"Harold is made up of first-rate people – kind, moral, sociable, hospitable, law-abiding and intelligent people, good enough and bright enough for any country. I confess to a cordial liking for them, and in this I am not at all singular."

A blacksmith eventually came, as well as a butcher and a painter, according to Harold newspaper clippings published in "Whispers From the Old West" by Mary Hall in 1993.

The paper chronicled other things – the first house built by W.G. Cowles in 1887, the Dilley and Findley jewelry store opening, Mrs. Reynolds giving birth to a 16-pound baby boy and a 4-year-old boy who died after being kicked in the head by a horse.

Harold

The newspaper, however, began to report the town's demise thereafter.

Of course, the railroad didn't come. The Methodist church burned down. On March 12, 1889, the newspaper reported that many people were leaving for Nebraska. In addition, in April 1889, people were leaving for Oklahoma.

By 1894, there were just 453 people in Harold's surrounding township, according to Millbrook's book. By the 1920s, little remained. The Harold House still stood, along with the jewelry store and the old Dilley home. The post office closed in 1891, according to the Kansas State Historical Society.

Meanwhile, Bill Miner's great-grandfather had never moved from Ness City, where he had his own business, Miner Brothers Co. – an abstract, title and farm and home insurance business the elder Miner started in 1885 and which Bill Miner runs today, Miner said.

William Miner also served as the Ness City mayor from 1887 to 1888. Bill Miner's great-uncle, Harold Miner, called Hal, was the second generation to run the business, along with Bill Miner's grandfather, Percy. His father, Alden, was the third generation, "and now it's me," he said.

There probably won't be a fourth generation, Miner said, noting his children have other interests. His great-uncle, Harold, also didn't have children who continued in the profession. Harold's son, Harold Craig Miner, was a noted Kansas historian and history professor at Wichita State University who wrote more than 40 books on local, regional and national history. Craig died in September 2010, leaving as one of his survivors, his eldest son, Harold Miner.

Bill Miner still has the original handbill proclaiming Harold a town.

"I don't know if they ever passed it out," he said with a chuckle, noting the misspelling of the word "beatiful" in the promotion.

Crumbling house, hunting lodge

These days, only a few remnants remain of Harold, which sits a mile west of Highway 283 and a mile north of the Hodgeman/Ness county line. That includes the jewelry store, now a barn; the hotel, which was renovated to a home; and the school, said Donnie Betz, 73, of Jetmore, who still owns land by the Harold town site – land his parents settled on in the mid-1930s.

Betz said the home site where he was born in 1937, a stone house on the edge of Harold, is falling in.

"I was the last one born there and one of the last ones who went to school there," Betz said, noting the school closed two years after he started.

He also said the creamery still stands a mile west and a mile south of the town site.

"On the inside, you can open the door and still see where it is tilted," Betz said of a typical creamery.

There once was a small cemetery, but when the town dissolved, the owner pulled up the graves and farmed over the land, he said.

Harold is now just a private farmstead and a winter hunting lodge owned by the Nuss family, said Susan Nuss. She didn't say much about the town, noting concerns about trespassing.

However, Nuss said,

"We really love the place. It is special."

Besides a hunting destination, Harold still gets a little statewide notoriety, Betz said.

"You still see it on TV when we have severe weather," he said.

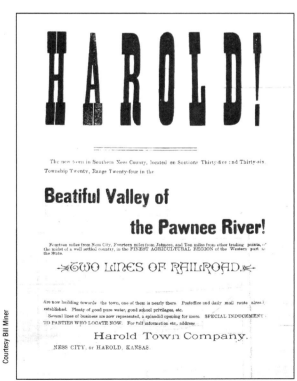

This is the original Harold handbill, complete with a misspelling. Bill Miner, whose great-grandfather helped found Harold, said it was among the family documents.

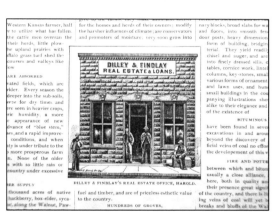

Town developers Dilley and Findley had a real estate business in Harold. The town was officially founded in May 1886 and peaked in 1887.

Cash City

❖ Clark County ❖

***This town's survival depended on the railroad.
But the railroad never came.***

He has found a few sardine containers and some square nails around the site where a few of his ancestors once lived, noting passers-by would never know the spot amid the Clark County prairie once was home to 500 people.

There were hotels and a blacksmith, shoe and wagon shops, a lumberyard and livery. Cash City even had a doctor, a drugstore and a mercantile, along with a newspaper, the Cash City Cashier, which told of the town's bright future.

Cash City might even rival a metropolis like Chicago, the paper reported.

"Her merchants are kept constantly on the move, barely having time to go to their meals," the editor wrote. "Vehicles crowd the streets and the farmers' wagons come and go away loaded."

Yet, traces of the once bustling town are a rarity – except for the books full of history his father passed to him, said Ford County Commissioner Kim Goodnight. Old Cash City, these days, is just a windmill in a pasture.

"The prairie has reclaimed everything," Goodnight said.

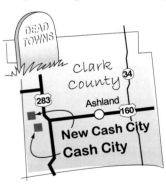

Location: Straight west of Ashland and about three miles west of U.S. 283/160.

'An opportunistic bunch'

In 1886, a man named Cash Henderson, with ties to Wichita, had a dream of a city at the intersection of the Tuttle, Ashland and Meade Center trails. Henderson got a post office in his town by June 1886, and the town sprang up.

Besides businesses, there was a school, church services and a literary club. The newspaper, The Cash City Cashier, published its first edition that October, spouting good things about the town's prospects for many issues.

An early edition from the Cash City newspaper promoted the town with hype.

One of the Seven Wonders! Infant of the Plains! Less than six months old with all the branches of business represented! Cash City certainly has a bright future in store. This beautiful and rapidly growing city, where but a short time ago roamed the buffalo and coyote, is situated in the western part of Clark County ... Everyone coming here sees at once the splendid field we have for a good town.

The paper told of a place where corn planted into the sod made 30 to 40 bushels an acre with the second year yields topping 60 bushels an acre. The paper reported the town would soon get a railroad, with the possibility of two more lines going through the city.

"What an opportunistic bunch these people were," Goodnight said. "They were doing this all on the premise that the railroad was coming through."

Western Kansas wasn't the easiest environment to homestead, either, he said. It was an area of few trees and few settlements. The land had never seen a plow.

"It was a very harsh environment to spring a town up on the middle of the prairie on the hope that the railroad would come through," he said. "And obviously, people were expecting it to profit."

Nevertheless, within six to eight months, the tone of the paper began to turn dismal. The town was no longer booming like its counterparts to the west, reporting that Cash City town lots were for sale at a discount.

In August 1887, with news that the railroad would not come through the city, Henderson and the group moved the town and most of the buildings a few miles northward in hopes of catching the tracks there.

The paper again tried to give promising hope.

"The Cashier has clung to Cash City with all sincerity through her gloomy days and now that smooth sailing is in sight, we have decided to tighten our grip. We have lost our location but not our name and acting as the Arab of old, we have 'quietly folded our tent and joined the procession.' And we shall sound the bugle as the procession progresses."

However, the planned extension never came. The railroad built a track to Englewood, 12 miles to the south, which was the end of the line. By 1888, the newspaper had dissolved, the businesses closed and most of the residents moved to nearby

Cash City

Ashland, the county seat.

By 1893, the town site was abandoned, most of the buildings torn down or moved. And by 1895, the Kansas Legislature official vacated Cash City.

Goodnight said his great-grandmothers, on both his father's and mother's sides, grew up around Cash City.

He recalls family outings to sites around the area, including Old Cash and New Cash cities. His father, Charles "Don" Goodnight, spent years recording the town's history. He died in 2000.

"I became the official family caretaker of all this information," Goodnight said.

The tradition continues, he said. Not long ago, he took his sons-in-law to the site.

"There's a spirit at the place – something that seems right," he said. "My father passed down that spirit."

Nothing left

When Kansas Secretary of Commerce Pat George, Dodge City, became good friends with Goodnight, it didn't take him long to realize he had something in common with the Ford County commissioner.

In the 1980s, before becoming a legislator and still single, George stayed in a home at Proffitt Lake on the property

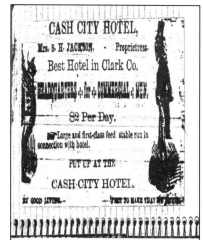

Various advertisements are seen in an old version of the Cash City Cashier newspaper.

where Old Cash City once sat. He watched the area for a landowner and used the pond to fish. He began learning about the area's history and began doing his own research, even taking a metal detector over the area.

He came across an old plat of the town, which he still has.

"It is such a beautiful part of the state – the rolling hills, the mesas," George said, noting he used to camp at St. Jacob's Well, a basin not far from the Cash City town sites.

It amazes him a town once blossomed then completely disappeared from existence – a town few even know existed.

"It's pretty sandy soil and, over 100 years, it's not hard to imagine" what remains being covered with sand, he said. "I often thought I should dig down four feet and see if I can find anything."

Thousands of towns across Kansas have met the same fate as Cash City, George said. Moreover, these days, there are others that are just trying to survive.

Serving as the Commerce Secretary under Gov. Sam Brownback, George said one project he planned to tackle was to help revitalize the rural landscape and turn the tide for Kansas' struggling small towns.

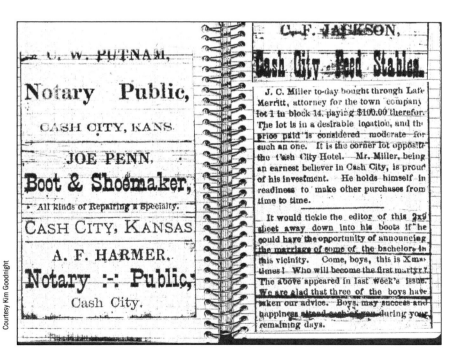

Good news was published in the Cash City Cashier about the promise for a town of 500, along with advertisements for local businesses. The Cashier's first edition was Oct. 29, 1886. It dissolved in 1888.

Sitka

❖ Clark County ❖

Professional rodeo cowboy and family are last residents in town.

Preparing to haul water to thirsty cattle during October's dry spell, professional steer wrestler Jule Hazen peered across a landscape where a lively town once stood.

An old bank – now a heaping pile of bricks – sits near the corner of the city street that leads to his ranch house. A few foundations are scattered in the neighboring pasture where cattle graze across sidewalks that lead to nowhere – signs that people once inhabited this farming and ranching community.

But not anymore.

Living in the nearly 100-year-old home he and his wife, Heidi, bought earlier this year, Hazen is the last cowboy in Sitka.

"My cousin said you can still see where the city blocks were at from the top of the elevator," Hazen said, gesturing to the town's last business, a cooperative open only during harvest seasons.

Those taking U.S. 183 to the Oklahoma border will find Sitka, Kansas, a small pit stop in southern Clark County. It seems the town, once a center of commerce, has quietly slipped away.

Location: Sitka is about a mile south of U.S. 160 on U.S. 183.

As cold as Sitka, Alaska

Eldora McMinimy, who lives on a farm just outside the city limits, said Sitka was once a thriving community. With the help of Ashland's Pioneer-Krier Museum, she published a book on Sitka's history in April, 2010.

Her husband's ancestors were among the area's early settlers, homesteading the land even before Sitka's first post office began in 1886. As the story goes, Sitka got its name from a fierce winter when temperatures dipped to 17 degrees below zero. A group of men had gathered to discuss what to name the town, and one suggested Sitka, saying, "It's as cold as Sitka, Alaska," McMinimy said.

Sitka's initial start, however, wasn't prosperous, she said.

The terrain rough and the cold, those trying to eke out a living off the prairie left. The post office closed in 1888. Still, others persevered and, by 1900, several families had established farms and ranches. The post office reopened in December 1908, and the town began to grow.

The Feb. 11, 1909, The Wichita Eagle reported, "A new Town to Rise on Old Site of Sitka." By October 1909, the Clark County Clipper reported that Sitka had a population of 41 – counting five pigs.

Growth continued, McMinimy said. Sitka boasted two lumberyards, a drugstore, a couple of groceries, plus elevators, livery barns, garages, a railroad, depot and hotel. A school had nearly 80 children in 1924.

One local resident told McMinimy she recalls as many as 300 people living in Sitka at one time, but McMinimy considers that number a little high. She does know that Sitka Township peaked at 559 residents in 1916. With the advent of railroad lines in other towns, Sitka began a slow decline.

One of Sitka's last stores closed in the late 1940s and another store closed in 1959 – both lost by fire. St. Mary's Church closed in 1957. The Methodist Church closed in 1953. The post office closed in 1964 and a service station in 1965.

Sitka's decline

In a Kansas City Star interview in 1995, former restaurant owner Buddy Probst, according to McMinimy's book, blamed Sitka's decline on the water situation.

"Sorriest water you ever drank," he told the reporter. "Hook it up to an ice-making machine, and it'd eat the tubing." Probst closed his restaurant, which he operated out of the old school, in 1999 – partly due to state regulation issues, McMinimy said, noting there were other reasons for the town's demise.

Transportation was a major reason, she said, noting the advent of cars made it easier for folks to travel to the county seat town of Ashland, just 7 miles away, for supplies.

Declining rural population also was a big factor, she said. The Dust Bowl took some of the region's farmers. Then, over the years, as farms began to grow larger, fewer farmers were farming more acres of land. Pickup trucks once used to haul grain to the elevator made way for grain trucks, which, today, have made way for primarily large tractor-trailers.

McMinimy said some people moved a few of the homes to

Sitka

An old abandoned home has nearly fallen down. There are just a few remains of Sitka, a Clark County town that once was thriving. Only one family stills lives in town.

Ashland, as well as the Catholic rectory and the Methodist parsonage. The depot was moved to Ashland, but now is at home at Dodge City's Boot Hill Museum.

Other buildings were torn down or burned down. A lane of trees still leads to the site of where St. Mary's Catholic Church once sat. The church collapsed in 1996. And the abandoned Methodist church burned to the ground in 2001. The school, once the home of Probst's restaurant, still stands, as well as a few dilapidated homes.

Trucks loaded with grain come in to dump at the elevator during the season. Old cisterns and well pumps are scattered about, including one near Hazen's home and one near the site of the Methodist church. A few sidewalks are still visible amid the grass and weeds.

In the distance, not far from Hazen's home, is a railroad bridge.

"The last train out of Sitka, loaded with wheat, left in Febru-

ary 1994," McMinimy writes. "The wrecking crews then removed the main line and siding tracks that crossed U.S. 183 at Sitka, piling old rail ties and other debris on and near the track."

The last folks in town

During the summer, Hazen stays busy traveling the rodeo circuit. But as fall approaches, the rodeo season is winding down, with Hazen working around the home and tending to cattle while his wife, Heidi, teaches school at nearby Ashland.

In December 2010, Hazen, who, at the time, was eighth in the nation for steer wrestling, competed in the National Finals Rodeo in Las Vegas – the Super Bowl of rodeo.

Meanwhile, there is growth occurring in Sitka, the cowboy adds with a grin. He and Heidi increased the population by one in 2011.

Eldora McMinimy stands by the Sitka road sign. She wrote a book about the town she's lived in since the late 1950s. The grain elevator, opened only during the harvest season, is the last business in town.

Hampton

❖ Rush County ❖

*Locals are preserving an old cemetery at the site
of this old fort road's dead town.*

Abandoned amid the post rock prairie, the small cemetery was overgrown with grass and the fence broken enough that cattle could wander through it. And today, except for the foundation of the nearby school and a stone post marking the site, the cemetery is all that is left of Hampton.

It seemed to be a town that had everything going for it. It was one of the first settlements – if not the first – in Rush County, situated first as a stop along the Fort Hays/Fort Dodge military trail. Eventually, it had several businesses, including a general store, a stage and blacksmith shop. Residents also had their eye on a railroad.

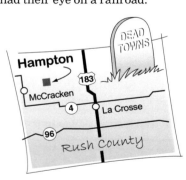

Carolyn Thompson recalls these facts from her home not far from the site – noting the piece of acreage that once had throngs of settlers isn't even visible anymore. With their dreams dashed, the residents moved away.

But Thompson, along with her nearby neighbor, Shirley Higgins, didn't want to see the story or the unkempt cemetery lost with time. With bodies and graves being moved by family members to well manicured plots in other towns, locals took action to begin a cleanup job of a forgotten piece of history. It also led the women to chronicle the newspaper accounts of Hampton's tale in the book they cowrote, "Hampton and the Big Timbers Valley."

Location: Five miles east and one mile north of Mc-Cracken

Being on a trail, "it does have such an interesting history," Thompson said.

Stop along a fort trail

Back in the 1860s, before railroad tracks would zigzag across Kansas, much of the only population in the western part of Kansas was merchants heading westward. Many at that time traveled the Santa Fe Trail that passed by Fort Larned, a Pawnee County fort established in 1859. Only a few pioneers were trying to eke out a living from the barren landscape.

With the advent of Fort Dodge and Fort Hays in the 1860s, the need for military supply trails grew, writes Larned historian David Clapsaddle in his timeline of the Fort Hays/Fort Dodge Road.

Gen. Winfield Scott Hancock, known for his force against Native Americans, once wrote, "My impression is that the real route of travel for emigrants here after will be from Fort Hays or Harker (most probably from Hays) directly across to some point a little west of Dodge, crossing Walnut Creek and branches of Pawnee Fork, where the country affords excellent grass, good running water, plenty of wood, good roads."

Soon after, an inspector general proposed a route between the two posts. That included a stop at Big Timbers crossing where the inspector wrote that the area had good water, grass and wood and "pools never failing," Clapsaddle's article reports.

Thompson figures there was some sort of ranch or outpost here in the early beginnings of the trail. And Clapsaddle records that in 1877, Monty Leach was appointed postmaster of the area, and he established a store.

"This provided the nucleus of a little community called Hampton, the official designation of the post office, so named for Joe Hampton, the area's first settler," Clapsaddle writes.

The town grew with Richard Mulroy building a two-story house and later establishing a hotel, according to Clapsaddle. Other businesses included the Nobel Bros. store, Billy Metz's blacksmith shop, a couple of stage companies and a school. There was a ball team the county paper called the Hampton Nines. Residents met regularly for church.

Life here was like any other town. The area paper reported on marriages, births and other happenings, according to the Hampton book. And by all accounts, it seemed the town was growing.

June 1878 – A store to be started at Hampton, Big Timber, by Mr. Crawford.

August 1883 –A game of baseball is on the program of the Harvest Home Picnic at Hampton the 15th.

1884 – A Mr. Updegraph of Hampton has invented a gun, which he claims will eclipse all other guns all ready manufac-

Hampton

tured for firing. He says that two hundred shots a minute can be fired. He left for Washington to have it patented. ... Mr. I. N. VanNordsrand killed a large bald eagle in Hampton Saturday last. It measured over 5 feet from wing tip to wing tip. Hampton is rapidly filling up with new settlers.

Residents were hopeful their community would grow into a metropolis of sorts. Moreover, they wished for a railroad, the newspaper articles proclaimed. Even when the town of Mc-Cracken appeared a handful of miles to the west, Hampton's colonists didn't give up hope. In 1886, a resident wrote this for the local paper.

It has been some time since we noticed anything in your valuable paper from this side of the county. We realize that it is our duty as patrons to help fill your column. Perhaps some of your old contributors think that Hampton is dead, but we are glad to inform you that they are mistaken.

We know that McCracken is in the lead, but we don't intend to let Hampton die. We are glad to see our neighboring cities boom but OLD HAMPTON WAS HERE FIRST!

Her name was recorded in the early history of Rush County. She has stood all the droughts, hot winds, perils and starvation which all had a tendency to drive away our support and cause us to become embarrassed, but the Hamptonites were men of courage, stamina and energy and stood by the old pioneer town. The railroad will be an advantage to Hampton. We will take new courage and become more and better satisfied that Hampton will live and flourish and be remembered as one of the pioneer centers in the early history of Rush County. Our valley is rich and fertile. There is not a spot of land that is better known in the east than Big Timber Valley.

However, for Hampton, life would be short, Clapsaddle writes. When nearby McCracken was organized with the coming of the railroad in 1886, Hampton began to die. The local storeowner ran his store another three to four years following McCracken's founding, but finally closed it down.

The government discontinued Hampton's post office in December 1887, although residents petitioned to have it re-opened, which happened a month later, according to the Hampton book.

In "Kansas: A Cyclopedia of State History," published in 1912, Hampton was still listed as a small hamlet.

Cemetery, foundations and a few ruts

Other ghost towns dot Rush County, towns with names like Shaffer, Hargrave and Loretto. Like those dead towns, Hampton, these days, is just a meager memory.

The school foundation remains, as well as a few wagon ruts from the old trail – that is, if a visitor knows where to look. Even the Big Timbers Creek rarely flows – except during heavy rains, said Hampton book coauthor Shirley Higgins.

James Start, who migrated from Utica, New York, and helped found Hampton, was Higgins' great-great grandfather – one reason she became interested in the little town.

Renovation of the cemetery occurred in the 1990s, which included building a new fence and installing stone posts, Thompson said.

Higgins said they had a man come out and douse for more graves, turning up an additional 132 unmarked burials. Volunteers put a cross on each site.

In completion of the renovations, they held a celebration in honor of the county's and trail's past, Higgins said.

This is a photo of Hampton's first school with its students. All that is left in Hampton is a cemetery.

Hampton and the Big Timbers Valley

Ash Valley

❖ Pawnee County ❖

Ash Valley is a ghost town on a ghost railroad

Daniel Kalal didn't know what he would find as he drove his motorcycle down the back roads from Wichita to his destination – a long defunct town on the western Kansas prairie.

His suspicions were there would be little, if anything, left of the once thriving railroad city of Ash Valley.

Kalal learned of the Pawnee County town from a co-worker whose ancestors had once lived there. He has traveled many a Kansas back road to several ghost towns, but he had never been to this spot.

Thus, one Friday, he jumped on his bike and began the journey westward.

"I thought I'd go there, park the bike and take a look," he said.

Pawnee County's youngest town

Ash Valley isn't an old town. Compare it to the likes of Kansas settlement in the 1870s and 1880s and most would consider it a youngling.

Although the town didn't rise until 1917 along the Anthony and Northern Railroad, residents had the same dreams as any town's founding fathers. They wanted to see it grow.

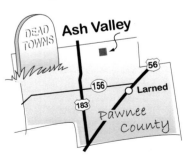

Location: Five miles east of Highway 183 and three miles south of the Pawnee/Rush county line.

Settlers were in the area as early as 1875, including Kyle Pieschl's great-grandparents who came to the Ash Valley area in 1877 and lived in a dugout not far from the future community. At that same time, the government established the Ash Valley Post Office, most likely in a resident's home a half-mile south of the present town site.

By 1886, locals had built the Pleasant Hill School, paying a teacher $33 a month for a four-month term. The same year, Methodists organized a church. With news of a railroad coming through the area, excitement developed for a new town.

The town was first called Ely, named after a Larned real estate man and landowner, according to a Feb. 13, 1967, article in the Pawnee County newspaper, The Tiller and Toiler. The

paper reported in a later edition that by the time the railroad had built through the area in 1917, entrepreneurs already were flocking to the new town. By 1919, the area school was moved to Ely and became a grocery, the newspaper reported.

Locals built a new school at a cost of $5,620. As other districts closed, the Ash Valley School had an enrollment of more than 40 students with two teachers offering grade and high school education.

Meanwhile, the post office, which the government had discontinued in 1908, was re-established inside the general store May 15, 1922.

But residents started to dislike Larned's Ely for some reason, said former resident Wilma Cook Creed, who, at 97, was born in a house at the site before the town was developed.

A Tiller and Toiler article said Ely's name change could have been related to a sensational criminal case in 1924 when Mary E. Eggleston, a widow, was convicted of attempting to murder businessman D. A. Ely, also a widower.

"The case became a hot issue when Eggleston appealed to Gov. Davis for pardon and 3,800 citizens signed petitions asking that the pardon not be granted. However, the pardon was granted and reaffirmed by the Kansas Supreme Court in April 1925," the newspaper reported.

How long it was named Ely is anyone's guess, said Pieschl, who is working to preserve the memories of Ash Valley.

A 1925 Tiller and Toiler article mentions the town's new name of Ash Valley and that the railroad had become the Wichita and Northwestern. At that time, the town had a bank, garage, lumberyard, an elevator, two general stores and a blacksmith shop, as well as other businesses.

Just like after the Civil War, developers used advertisements to try to sell the town, including one by the bank that boasted, "Kansas grows the best wheat in the world – the Ash Valley territory grows the best wheat in Kansas."

According to the Tiller and Toiler article, in 1924, the elevator shipped 250 carloads of wheat from the town. One of the newspaper's reporters predicted a prosperous future for the little wheat capital.

"With its favorable situation in a wide, fertile territory, its substantial growth from year to year is a foregone conclusion."

Creed, born in what she described as "a four-room prairie house" in 1913, said there used to be many similar houses when she was growing up.

Ash Valley

She recalls attending the local Pleasant Hill Methodist Church and going to 4-H club meetings at the school. She tells a story of the town's banker, who was up on a windmill on a windy day and was blown off – dying from the injuries.

In the 1920s, according to a Tiller and Toiler article, there were more than 100 people living at Ash Valley. Nevertheless, the town began a gradual decline there after. Residents began traveling to Larned to do business. The bank liquidated, probably during the Great Depression, Pieschl speculates.

By 1941, the railroad officials abandoned the line, as well.

"My dad remembers walking down the railroad tracks around World War II watching the crews tearing it out for the war," Pieschl said.

The post office closed in 1941 and the school, with just three pupils, closed in 1962, the Toiler reported. One of the students, a senior, was the last to graduate from the school.

What remained of the elevator was razed in 1967. The church, destroyed by lightning in 1944, was rebuilt out of brick. It closed in 2001.

Ghost town on a ghost railroad

These days, Ash Valley is nothing more than a ghost town on a ghost railroad with just a few remnants of the past lingering. Kalal's motorcycle trip, at first, took him to a barren spot in the road – the GPS markings for the town off by about a mile or so.

He soon spotted the school, as well as the well-maintained church and the brick remains of one of the garages.

Pieschl, who grew up four miles from Ash Valley and now works for a Great Bend landscaping business, said he felt too

This photo shows a Wichita Northwestern train engine and cars near a water tank at Ash Valley. The photo was taken in 1917.

www.kansasmemory.org

passionate about the town to see what remained fall to ruin. He owns the church and the school, as well as the two remaining houses – one of which was his grandparents' home. He doesn't know what he will do with the school, but he wants to keep the roof and windows in repair so it will not cave in.

The church is now a community center with more than 70 members who pay an annual due to help maintain it. Four times a year, the members gather for fellowship, such as birthday celebrations, potlucks and, at Christmas, worship. Pieschl also rents out the building for gatherings.

Another relic is about a mile east of town, a limestone marker honoring a man who died before Kansas was a state.

Cliff Line, a former resident of Ash Valley, was digging a posthole in 1916 when he hit a rock, according to a Hutchinson News article from the time. When he unearthed it, he found lettering on it and realized it was a grave from 75 years earlier. The stone said: A.D. 1841 June W.D. Silverton Shot with (below shows the carving of an arrow).

Pieschl said the railroad erected a monument that still stands today along the former railroad line.

These are just some of the memories that linger, he said.

Creed, who now lives with her son, Doyle, at Little River, said some of her best memories at Ash Valley included wearing overalls and working on 4-H projects at the school. 4-H she said, helped her in college, when she and six other women founded a sorority, Alpha of Clovia, at Kansas State University in 1931. The women were looking for an economical place to live while attending college during the beginnings of the Great Depression.

The 4-H scholarship house is still in existence today and celebrated 80 years in spring 2011.

Photos by Amanda Loman/The Hutchinson News

Above: Native Kyle Pieschl owns the schoolhouse and is trying to keep it from deteriorating too much by making sure the windows and roof are in good condition.

Left: Pieschl stands in front of the church in what was once the community of Ash Valley. The church and nearby schoolhouse are now owned by Pieschl and the church now functions as a community center with 70 members.

Zook

❖ Pawnee County ❖

**University of Kansas All-American and
NFL great John Zook was a product of Zook, Kansas.**

Gerald Bowman pointed to a sea of grass in the distance, saying it once was the gridiron where he played halfback.

It's also where University of Kansas All-American and NFL player John Zook played his first high school game before Zook High School closed for good after Bowman's graduation in 1962.

These days, little remains of what once was a small football powerhouse amid the plains of Pawnee County. Just one brick pillar still stands at the old school, which is now a hole full of trash. Swings on the rusted schoolyard swing set creak in the wind and the gymnasium, with its brick façade on the front, is used as a farm shed.

Nevertheless, for Bowman and his brother, Benny, the memories of playing sports in the little town still linger.

"We would go undefeated in six man and undefeated in eight man," said Gerald Bowman, 66, of Macksville, who had his own successful post-high school career at Hutchinson Community College before finishing his football eligibility at Fort Hays State University. "In the early 1950s, we were ranked in the top 10 for six-man in the nation."

Location: Zook is a half-mile east of Highway 19 on 972 Road in Pawnee County.

Where is Zook?

Bowman once told a reporter at The News during his time at HCC that most classmates didn't believe him when he told them he was from Zook, Kan. There just couldn't be a town with such a name, they would say.

"I used to carry a map with me," Bowman told The News in 1965, "but that didn't help much. Some people would see the town on the map and still not believe it."

Even Russ Ringsak, who works with Garrison Keillor's "A Prairie Home Companion," poked a little fun at Zook in 2005

after a visit to the Kansas State Fair – mimicking what Bowman might have felt like on occasion.

It's your first day in the college dorm in the big city and someone asks where you're from and you have to say, "I'm from Speed, Kansas." Or "I'm from Gross." "Um, my hometown is Narka. It's in Kansas." A sense of humor would be a handy thing to take along if you were from a place with a name like Gas or Studley. Either that or a good counter offensive. For example: "Zook? Zook, Kansas? What kind of name is that for a town? Zook? You gotta be kiddin'." "What, you never heard of Zook? Where you been, anyway? Everybody knows about Zook. Zook is, like, very cool. Zook is, like, a synonym for 'cool.' You look up 'cool' in the dictionary and there's a picture of Zook. Zook is an Indian word that means 'cool.' You're the first person I ever met in my whole life that hadn't heard of Zook. Everybody in the freakin' world knows about Zook."

Zook isn't an Indian name, however. Moreover, Zook is situated not quite a mile east of North K-19 in southeast Pawnee County. David Zook, who still lives in town, said his ancestors were of Mennonite descent, which included a man named John Zook. He came on a train to Larned with his seven sons and three daughters in the mid-1880s and then migrated to what would be the area known as Zook.

According to Zook history provided by Benny Bowman, the town of Zook didn't materialize until 1916. Folks formed the town amid the construction of the Anthony and Northern Railroad through the area.

David Zook said they considered calling the new town Chesterman after the man from whom they purchased the town site. However, there already was a Chester, Kansas, and so they named it Zook because they purchased land from Jake Zook to build the railroad.

Thus, a little town was born, complete with a small grocery, a bank, a lumberyard and elevators. In 1921, residents from several area school districts decided to consolidate the one-room schools that were scattered about the region. In 1922, Zook Union No. 4 District opened, becoming one of the first consolidated schools in western Kansas.

The school was built at a cost of $58,000.

But Zook never took off. As more people purchased cars and roads improved, more residents went to Larned to bank and get groceries. In 1941, the railroad quit running, the tracks were torn up and the elevators were sold.

On May 4, 1950 – the same evening young people were gathered in the high school gymnasium for the prom – a tornado came through and destroyed a bus garage, a shop building, a home and other structures, Benny Bowman said. The school would hang on another 12 years before it closed for good.

School was town's center

Despite the town's lack of growth, the school was the social center for locals who cheered on the Zook Bulldogs during each sports season. So was the case in 1947 when Zook played in the "unofficial state six-baller championship" against Hudson High School in Hutchinson, according to a November 1947 edition of The News.

Hudson coach John Paden challenged any team in the state for the six-man championship, making particular efforts to get Montezuma, Argonia and Offerle – all known powerhouses. While those teams, however, wouldn't accept the challenge, Zook did.

Zook ended up losing to the undefeated team 13-0, but held Hudson to its lowest margin of victory.

In 1952, the school built a new auditorium/gymnasium. In 1953, when Benny Bowman was a freshman, the Zook Bulldogs were a nationally ranked six-man team, finishing the season undefeated.

Younger brother Gerald Bowman was a natural athlete as well. He spent his high school summers working for Dan Zook, David Zook's father.

"That was my weightlifting," Gerald Bowman said with a chuckle. His senior year, Bowman helped lead the team that included the young John Zook.

Then he graduated in 1962 – one of 11 classmates. When they walked across the gym that spring, they had no idea they'd be the last class to do so, Bowman said. That summer, John Zook decided to go to Larned to school. Others followed. When school started the next fall, there weren't enough students to have a school. The high school closed and the teachers hired for the year received their full salary even though they hadn't taught a day.

The grade school continued until the spring of 1968. Then the three-story brick building was closed for good.

The gymnasium was purchased and much of the insides torn out, said A.W. Schartz, a retired Zook-area farmer who now lives at Larned and owns the structure to store his farm machinery. The man who first purchased it also tried to get the gym floor torn up, but realized it would be too much work.

"It still has the free throw lines and the center circle," Schartz said.

David Zook said the school eventually was razed. Someone purchased the bricks to build an apartment complex in Larned.

"The community was oriented around the school activities," David Zook said. "When something was going on, all the community just showed up. When the school closed, there were two little churches in the community. They stayed for awhile, but those closed eventually, too." Those community gatherings were fond for Gerald Bowman as well.

"One of the biggest things I remember about Zook is all the people would bring potluck to the gym at the end of the school year and then all the high school kids would take on the farmers in a game of baseball," he said.

The school memories still live on, David Zook said. Each May, the Zook High School reunion commences in Zook.

Home of an All-American

Besides playing college ball, Gerald Bowman taught high

Amy Bickel/The Hutchinson News

Gerald Bowman, 66, of Macksville, graduated from Zook High School in 1962.

school history and physical education, as well as served as a school administrator in Macksville.

He also coached for several years, leading the Sharon High School in Barber County to the eight-man football state championship in 1976.

In April, Bowman browsed around the Zook community room where rows of trophies line a glass case and the walls are covered in senior class pictures and other photos. The building used to be the high school shop. The local Extension Home Unit raised funds to turn it into a community center.

Included in the case is Bowman's senior year football team picture, which includes John Zook. He was tall and athletic, Bowman recalls, adding that even a little town like Zook can produce an outstanding athlete.

John Zook was a three-year letterman at the University of Kansas, picked twice for all conference honors and anchored one of the top defensive units for the university. He was an honorable mention All-American in 1967 and a consensus All-American in 1968, helping lead the team to the 1968 Orange Bowl – the year KU was named No. 6 by The Associated Press.

KU coach Pepper Rodgers called him "the most full speed player on every snap that you could imagine." Zook ended his career with 202 tackles – fourth all-time for a KU defensive lineman.

The Los Angeles Rams, in the fourth round of the 1969 NFL draft, chose Zook. He eventually ended up with the Atlanta Falcons, where he began his NFL career in 1969. He played 144 games and was a second-team All-Pro selection in 1973 and was voted to the 1973 Pro Bowl. In 1976, the Falcons traded him to the St. Louis Cardinals where he finished his career.

Bowman said John Zook occasionally comes back to the area where his brothers still farm, though Bowman hasn't seen his classmate in years.

David Zook said he always cheered on his cousin, although he never was a KU fan.

"I always wanted him to play well, but I always wanted him to get beat, too," he said with a laugh.

From The Hutchinson News, Nov. 21, 1947
Hudson beats Zook 13-0

The weatherman probably put sixball game promoter John Paden behind the eight-ball Thursday night for only a couple of hands full of fans turned to see Hudson highs' undefeated and united team score a 13-0 victory over Zook high in the first sixman football game ever presented in Hutchinson.

Those fans who did brave wet, drizzly and cold winds to see their first sixball game probably are agreed that the game's inventor was successful in his ambition to create a wide-open game.

Zook and Hudson teams raced from one end of the field to thee other. Zook high tossed 24 passes. Hudson split the air lanes for 14, making a total of 38 for the game.

While only nine of the aerials were completed, the clock stopped with every toss and it was difficult for fans to realize the teams were playing only 10-minute quarters and the game, which offered only 40 minutes of actual playing time, was two hours in the playing, start to finish.

Hudson got its scoring licks in early.

Midway in the first quarter, D. Searle, Hudson's great 195-pound fullback, broke away behind some smooth blocking for a 42-yard touchdown run. Exactly two minutes later, Hudson scored again on a 10-yard pass from Brensing to Alpers.

Hudson kicked off, Bowman returned to the 25. Pfister was rushed on a pass and he cut the ball loose straight into the arms of Searle who plowed back for 10 yards. Two running plays put the ball on the ten and Brensing tossed an easy one to Alpers for the touchdown. ...

From the first quarter on, it was a near even ball game. Early in the second quarter, Searle raced 75 yards and into the end zone only to have the field-length touchdown play called back because of clipping by a teammate.

The Hudson boys worked their way to the Zook three-yard line late in the quarter, but a pass interception ended the drive. That was the last serious scoring threat. Zook outplayed Hudson in the third quarter and staged one 48-yard march before losing the ball on a pass interception.

Zook held the Hudson team to its lowest margin victory in an all-victorious season. Hudson registered its ninth straight triumph and fans of that community are now claiming an unofficial state sixball championship.

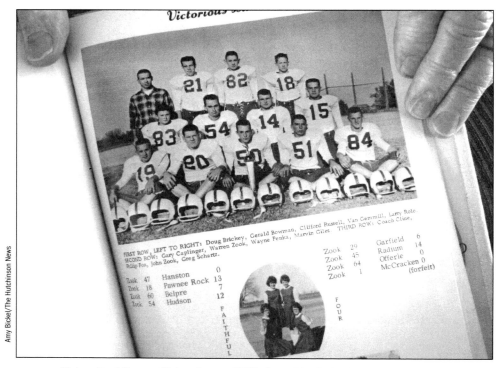

Amy Bickel/The Hutchinson News

University of Kansas All-American and NFL player John Zook played for the Zook High School football team his freshman year. He is in the back row, No. 82. Gerald Bowman, who also played football in college, is No. 20.

Nettleton

❖ Edwards County ❖

Town, founder succumbed to tragic circumstances

The old mansion still sits near the banks of the dry Arkansas River – one of the only remains of this town with a tragic tale.

And somewhere nearby, amid the once elaborate plantation, three unmarked graves of the home's former owners rest – the exact location forgotten with time.

Edwards County has several extinct towns – towns like Charlet, Ardell, Wendell and Centerview, said Ted Taylor, curator of the Edwards County Historical Society Museum in Kinsley. Founders of these trading posts had big ideas that their little communities would someday become a county seat and a prosperous metropolis, only to watch them disappear from the map.

Often, however, it is the little town of Nettleton Taylor thinks about, which carries perhaps the most catastrophic saga of them all – where a rich man's dreams were shattered by plagues, poverty and eventually death.

"We think about it every time we go to Larned," he said, noting the town is just five or six miles northeast of Kinsley on U.S. 56, right at the Edwards/Pawnee county line.

A man's demise

John Fitch, a wealthy man from Chicago, wanted to establish a plantation in Kansas, according to a book by local historian Myrtle Richardson. Around 1874, he purchased land that included the settlement of Nettleton, a town formed by the Santa Fe Railroad and named after a railroad official. Fitch changed the name to Fitchburg and, with visions of a big city growing up, he began spending a fortune on his plantation.

Larned's Tiller and Toiler newspaper from Feb. 11, 1916 stated Fitch had materials shipped from Chicago for his estate, which was equipped with plumbing and all conveniences.

"Even a gasoline lighting plant was installed – a wonder at that day…and probably the first of the kind in Kansas," the newspaper reported.

The home also served as a hotel of sorts for a doctor and others, Taylor said. According to a Kansas Historical Quarterly from 1940, Fitch raised corn, barley, millet, sweet potatoes, cabbage, tomatoes and other products, and became postmaster and railroad station agent. For a while, there seemed to be no limit to his ambitions and energy. He even had a flourmill operated by both steam power and windmills.

Disaster, nevertheless, pursued him. According to the Larned newspaper, grasshoppers came and drought hit. The prolonged droughts caused settlers to move from the community. Fitch's mill stopped grinding and Fitch watched as his once wealthy fortune dwindled away.

"Finally, to provide his family with the necessities of life, he had to engage in manual labor," the newspaper wrote. "He had lost all his property, save a little stretch of land along the river. This he was trying to redeem by hard labor.

Fitch would not give up, the Toiler reported.

"His fortune gone, his mill lost, his plantation project abandoned, his mansion practically deserted, Fitch was still plucky and determined yet to win."

An infant daughter died in fall 1877. But plagues continued to hit. In spring 1878, his wife died of cancer.

Fitch, 52, died July 25, 1878 from injuries received in a farming accident.

"On Monday, while Mr. John Fitch was raking hay with a sulky rake, his horses ran away and threw him from his seat before the rake," according to the July 18, 1978 edition of the Edwards County Leader. "One of the prongs of the rake struck him in the side inflicting a severe wound."

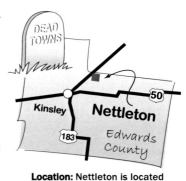

Location: Nettleton is located about five miles northeast of Kinsley, just off of U.S. 56 near the Edwards/Pawnee county line.

All were buried in the front lawn of the magnificent home. Fitch and his wife left four children, who eventually sold the mill and moved to Kinsley before moving on.

His obituary in the Kinsley Graphic said he was a lawyer by profession and editor of a newspaper before coming to Nettleton. During the Civil War, he had the position of Judge Advocate. He also authored "Annals of the Army of the Cumberland."

Nettleton survived for a while after the Fitches' deaths. The post office came in 1877 to what was then named Fitchburg, the Tiller and Toiler reported. However, locals didn't like the name because of prejudice against Fitch, who was "regarded as

Nettleton

high-toned." They petitioned the government and the name changed back to Nettleton.

The post office officially changed to Nettleton in February 1878. Nettleton, however, continued to struggle. The town had a hotel, a livery, general store, creamery, coal business and, eventually, in the early part of the 20th century, a school. Yet, in 1882, the post office closed, according to the Kansas State Historical Society. It reopened in 1903, only to close again in 1904.

The town seemed to be on the verge of bouncing back in the early teens. The post office opened again in 1912, although it closed by 1917 and never re-opened again. Locals built a two-story brick school in 1915 at a cost of $15,000, but it closed in 1943 and was razed, the bricks used to build a church in Pawnee County, according to The Hutchinson News.

Kinsley businessman and local historian John Ploger said his mother taught at the school in the late 1920s. She lived at a home at Nettleton during the week and then drove back to Kinsley on weekends.

Taylor said the population probably never peaked above 50, noting that the railroad was responsible for the town's population.

A mansion remains

Not much is left of this former aristocrat's dream. The graves are probably there, Taylor said, although many have searched for the exact location over the years and never found it.

Cement bases are all that remain of grain elevators in the town of Nettleton.

Amanda Loman/The Hutchinson News

There are old foundations of where the school once sat, as well as a cement slab for the ranch's bunkhouse. An old rickety bridge that once crossed the river was torn out some time during mid-century.

And, of course, there is the mansion. Or, as owner Leroy Gier says, he presumes it is the three-story mansion. A long-distance cousin of Fitch once stopped by in the late 1980s, he said. He had blueprints of the house.

"It came right out to the exact footage," Gier said.

Gier also farms around a few of the old foundations of the elevator, noting that Fitch would grind the flour, put it in railroad cars and ship it to the east. Even the old railroad is gone, he said.

There's still a sign marking the location, however, which lists the population as one.

As the last resident in Nettleton, Gier has heard many stories of the town and the Fitches, including the claim that relatives exhumed the bodies. But they are just stories, he said.

"There are no records," he said. "Just what people have passed down."

❖❖❖

Amanda Loman/The Hutchinson News

Nettleton's sole resident, Leroy Gier, stands by the county sign along U.S. 56. Gier owns the home which was most likely the three-story mansion built by John Fitch in the 1870's.

Edwards County Historical Museum

Nettleton's general store is seen in this photo. The store is no longer standing.

Hopewell

❖ Pratt County ❖

Once the home of NFL lineman Ollie Spencer,
Norman Rockwell-like Hopewell is no longer

These days, this tiny town has more sheep than people. It sits in the northwest corner of Pratt County, just across the road from Terry Smith's sheep pens. Yet, except for a few houses and an old church, the town where Smith grew up is nearly gone.

Not that residents didn't have hope for Hopewell. Its beginnings were similar to those of many a town that dots the Kansas landscape.

There was a school and church, stores and people. Nevertheless, as people began driving longer distances to go to work and do business, little Hopewell began to disappear.

It's sad, Smith said. For Hopewell, he said, was more than a town. It was a community.

"Residents would gather in (the store) every day," Smith said of one of the last businesses in town. "You'd get your mail; pop was a dime a bottle. Farmers would congregate there during the day to visit with their neighbors."

Hope for Hopewell

Just how the town was labeled the name Hopewell is anyone's guess, said local farmer Greg Giles.

However, Hopewell started in 1904 as a post office. The post office closed in 1908. The post office again opened by 1916, with the town taking the name of Fravel. The Fravel post office changed to Hopewell in 1921.

The town soon began to grow, springing up with the Anthony and Northern Railway, which had incorporated in 1912 and began to build tracks from Iuka to Pawnee County.

Ninety-one-year old Geraldine McAhren, of Byers, who grew up in Hopewell and is Giles' aunt, said the Farmer's State Bank of Hopewell opened for business about the same time as the name change.

The town also had a general store, a hotel, elevators, a blacksmith, a hardware store and lumberyard. The bank housed the post office until it closed in the mid-1920s, she said.

Fun included going to school and church, McAhren said. Other fond memories were of local couple, Roy and Mina Hodson, who had befriended her. She would sit on their laps at church and, when she was older, was in a quartet with Roy.

Other activities included rabbit hunts, writes Kansas ghost town author Daniel Fitzgerald. For instance, Hopewell's two lodges had a wager for an oyster dinner to see who could get the most rabbits. The winning team corralled more than 700 rabbits and herded them to a buyer at Byers. The buyer paid 75 cents each for jackrabbits and 35 cents a piece for cottontails.

Yet, while there were signs of prospering in the beginning, little Hopewell never took off.

When he was little, 20 or 30 people were living in or around Hopewell, Giles said. Today there is just a handful.

Giles, 57, said his father attended the small school, but it was closed by the time he could go there. The train also pulled up its tracks in the early 1940s. The post office closed in 1973, at the same time that his great aunt, postmistress Emily Pike – who also ran the general store – retired.

Giles recalls riding his bicycle to the general store to get a pop or a candy bar. It was one of those places out of a Norman Rockwell picture, where men gathered inside in front of the stove or he'd find them whittling outside when the weather was nice.

Pike's store had groceries and hardware and customers could even buy sandwiches, Giles said. Pike would slice the meat right in her store.

"It was a good community," he said. "There wasn't a house that I hadn't been in where I didn't have cookies and milk – and these were the fresh-baked ones. One woman would even make doughnuts."

He lived there all his life, Giles said. His grandparents moved to the Hopewell area to farm around 1924, making him the third generation to call the Hopewell community home. Now he is one of the last nearby.

The Greensburg tornado also went near Hopewell, he said. His father, who was in the basement of their rural residence with Giles' mother, died as a result of the tornado. His mother moved to Pratt.

Location: At the intersection of NW 140th and 110th Street in Pratt County.

Hopewell

Memories

The cemetery sits on the hill, and Terry Smith said he turned the old school into a barn around 1990. Otherwise, little remains of tiny Hopewell.

There is, however, a white church with the pile of rubble sitting in front of it. Out-of-state hunters want to turn the old Quaker church into a hunting lodge, said 81-year-old Wilbert Bevan, who moved to town in 1954. Nevertheless, the pile has been there for years.

"I put a sign out by it once," Bevan said, telling people to take what they wanted. Nothing has moved, however.

Hopewell had one claim to fame, Giles said. Ollie Spencer, an NFL lineman for nine years in the 1950s and 1960s who also served as the Oakland Raiders' offensive line coach for 17 years, grew up in Hopewell. He was born in 1931.

Giles said he misses the close-knit community that Hopewell once was – recalling folks would drop by his grandparents' house on a Sunday afternoon in the 1950s just to visit and watch television. They purchased the community's first set in 1953.

"It is a place you can't go back to," Giles said. "Memories are all you've got."

❖❖❖

Photos by Amanda Loman/The Hutchinson News

Above: The Hopewell Cemetery rests atop of a hill near the town site of Hopewell, which now has just a few residents left.

Left: One of the few structures still standing in Hopewell is a church. Someone started to renovate it, putting a pile of rubble on the curb. However, progress has stopped for now.

Sun City

❖ Barber County ❖

*Revived bar includes good eats, cold beer and good conversation
thanks to contractor who took a risk.*

It's a weekday afternoon in this little Gyp Hills town where population has waned to just 53 people - a town that these days is marked by a boarded-up bank, dilapidated storefronts and abandoned homes.

It's a town where dreams over the years have faded to oblivion.

Yet it's here in Sun City that Barber County rancher Kenton Marsh is in search of a cold bottle of beer and a good conversation.

In fact, jokes Sally Goldman, who provides the beer and small talk from across the bar on this spring day, there's not many a day Marsh doesn't stop by.

Maybe it's the atmosphere, which mirrors the likes of this cowboy town isolated in the red hills, not far from a gypsum mine. There's nothing fancy here, after all, with its wooden floors and hunting trophies on the walls.

Yet, it is iconic. A World War II veteran with a wooden leg, Buster Hathaway, along with his wife, Alma, purchased the place from his grandparents in 1946, Marsh said. For years, Buster served up frosty fishbowls of beer from an establishment where the only bathroom was an outhouse. When all the other places in town closed, Buster kept his doors open - the sort of place that caused main street Sun City to become packed with pickup trucks on a Saturday night.

In fact, it's said Buster's was the first bar in the state to serve draft beer - the longtime owner preferring Coors.

Marsh reminisces these facts but adds he was a bit worried as he watched the place he frequents go from owner to owner after Hathaway died in 1996 - 50 years after he opened the establishment. Hathaway's son, Steve, tried to make it go, as well as other owners. Then the place closed.

"I didn't know what would happen," Marsh said, but added he didn't have to wait long.

By August, Buster's was back in business, and the 60-year-old, in his cowboy hat and Wranglers, again rests on one of the original bar stools after a day on the ranch - leaning up to the bar and quenching his thirst on any Tuesday through Saturday.

"The water is hard, so you have to come and drink beer," Marsh said with a grin before taking another drink.

From suburbs to small town

Gary Goldman admits he was a bit skeptical when a friend,

who has several investments in the area, including large sections of ranchland, told him he bought a bar in Sun City, Kansas.

Goldman, a Florida contractor, had been to the town before to hunt.

"I came out here and told him he was crazy," Goldman says with a laugh as he stands in his restaurant kitchen, which nearly always smells of smoked meat.

But there was something about the place that Goldman couldn't quite shake. His friend told him he'd open the bar no matter what.

Goldman's son, Graham, told him he should take the chance. So Gary, his wife, Sally, and Graham left their busy lifestyle and suburban home near Orlando and moved to remote, slower-paced rural Kansas a year ago in April.

His friend owns the property while the Goldmans operate the bar and grill. For several months, they worked to get the place back in shape, which included newer bathrooms, a better kitchen and fixing up the bar area. By August, customers again were ordering fishbowls of beer along with steaks, prime rib and meats from the smoker.

Location: Near the intersection of River Road and Sun City Road.

Graham, who lives in an apartment on the back of the structure with his dog, Moose, typically runs the bar, Goldman said. While Goldman does much of the smoking, getting up sometimes as early as 4 a.m. to put meat on, Sally makes all the sides and desserts. Goldman said he wants to start catering from the tavern as well.

"Everything is homemade here," Sally Goldman said. "We don't open a can and pour it out."

Customers did notice some changes, Goldman said. Some items from Buster's day were sold long ago. But he and his wife were able to salvage the bar stools, parts of the bar, some booths and the wooden floor, which still has the worn look of

Sally Goldman talks with Kenton Marsh at the bar at Buster's in Sun City.

Photos by Sandra J. Milburn/The Hutchinson News

being treaded by boots and spurs.

A couple of Hathaway's bobcats still frequent the joint, but the stuffed rattlesnake had to go, Goldman said, noting Hathaway used to raise rattlesnakes in the old bank building and his wooden leg came in handy.

Goldman also learned quickly what the top seller would be on the menu.

"You have to have hamburgers and steaks," he said. "You're not going to sell much chicken around here."

Amid the Gyp Hills

"This is God's country," Marsh exclaimed as he pointed out the scenery from the bar window.

Those who travel the back roads of Barber County know what Marsh is talking about - a place where the sky expands across red hills that rise and fall like waves across a sea of grass.

And these rugged Gyp Hills are far from the supposed flat Kansas landscape.

It's where cattle roam in the summer until herded by cowboys, where good roads mean taking a path through a fence and crossing a grate into an open cattle range. Green cedars dot the butte-like terrain where the windswept grasses give way to prairie flowers.

These roads take travelers through places like Sun City, a virtual ghost town. They say there once were hundreds of people living in Sun City. There even once was a rodeo that drew folks from far and wide, Marsh said.

Sun City had two hotels, three livery barns, two dry-goods stores, three groceries, a bank, a hardware store and even a shoe shop among its commerce. But these days, the town of just 53 – a drop off of nearly 30 people since the 2000 census – and it continues to dwindle.

Buster's, however, lives on, serving hamburgers, steaks and smoked meats five days a week to the sound of spurs clanging regularly on the bar's hardwood floor. And recently, a craft shop opened up across the street on weekends as folks swarm to town.

That's enough for Goldman's mustache-covered lips to curl up in a smile.

"I love it," Goldman said of the new lifestyle. "I love this small community, and we're fitting in good."

Buster's is a bar and grill along the Main Street in Sun City where all their food is homemade and their specialty is smoked meats.

Lake City

❖ Barber County ❖

Amid the Gyps Hills, Lake City is the perfect setting for an aging ghost town.

It was a town crisis when the Lake City Bank began to fall into the street.

From her 120-year old ranch house, Carol Lake Rogers recalls the day, noting the old green stoves that toppled into the pile of rubble from the upstairs were "probably worth a few dollars."

These days, just part of the old bank still stands, looking like an open Barbie playhouse. An old bathroom sink hangs on a wall in the upper story, becoming visible after a portion of the building crumbled down. It's enough to cause Rogers to sigh in disappointment, saying that the town her great-grandfather, Reuben Lake, founded amid the scenic Gyp Hills cattle country is slowly chipping away.

Rogers is one of the last Lakes in Lake City, a Barber County town so remote there isn't a direct route to it. The paths are those less traveled – either dirt or a county road called River, which winds with the Medicine River all the way into Kiowa County.

The community at one time boasted a school, two groceries, a hardware store and a hotel, as well as more than 1,000 residents in and around its vicinity. All those businesses closed years ago, their buildings either shells of a former life or broken into shambles.

Moreover, Rogers estimates, there can't be much more than 50 people surrounding the town.

"It's sad to see these little towns go," she said. "When autos got plentiful, there was really no reason for people to stay here."

An old ranching town

Sitting in the home her grandfather, Riley, built for his first wife in 1886, a beautiful stone ranch home on the edge of the city, Rogers calls herself the keeper of Lake City's archives. While she didn't grow up in town, her parents sent her to live with her grandmother and Riley Lake's second wife, Pearl Lake, in the ranch home when school was out for the summer.

Rogers said Reuben Lake and his band of seven other men rode to the Gyp Hills to take advantage of the government's Homestead Act, which granted each 160 acres if they improved the land.

"My grandfather, Riley, who was 10 years old at the time, drove one of the wagons," Rogers said.

With some hostility still coming from the area's Native Americans, the small colony went back to northern Kansas for a short period, returning sometime in 1873. That's when the town began to form, thriving as a commerce center for those who farmed and ranched amid Barber County's hills and valleys, Rogers said, noting her great-grandfather had a sawmill by the river for a while, until it burned down.

Reuben Lake also served as Lake City's first postmaster, as well as Barber County's first sheriff.

Lake City, the site of it rather, was discovered by Reuben Lake in April, 1873. It is situated in Lake township, in the heart of the stock region, eighteen miles northwest of Medicine Lodge, with which is connected by a daily stage and mail line.

Its natural location is all that could be desired. In a deep valley, backed on the north by the bluff that rises above it, with the Medicine River, fringed with a dense growth of forest trees on the south, it is very beautiful.

– Medicine Lodge Cresset, March 2, 1900.

Lake City, it seemed, was prospering with two groceries, a blacksmith, a hardware store, a hotel and the bank. A post office opened in December 1873 and, at one time, Rogers said, it served more than 1,000 residents in a small area around the city. There also was a gas station, grain elevators, a telephone company, livery stables and a high school. There even was a doctor and a drugstore, she said.

Ronnie Hoagland, who lives in town and still operates the family ranch in the area, resides in the home he bought 40 years ago for just a few thousand dollars. He recalls when the school was open, the gas station was a fuel stop and farmers hauled their grain to a now-abandoned elevator.

His daughter, Kim, said she used to get money to buy fudgesicles at the local grocery.

The grocery, however, has been gone for years, she said.

Location: Lake City is located on River Road in Barber County.

Lake City

Lake City today

The hills and trees, mixed in with several abandoned buildings and homes, make Lake City the perfect setting for an aging ghost town.

Only a few structures remain of Lake City, remnants Rogers is amazed are still standing.

An old Gano elevator sticks up amid the weeds and trees in the center of a city block – right along the lines of the abandoned railroad track. The old blacksmith shop is wide open – a couple of plastic lawn chairs sit up on the concrete base. Some homes are abandoned and the old school has been closed for years.

Three old gas station pumps sit side-by-side in front of the boarded-up shop. There is also an old red pay phone, which, amazingly, still has a dial tone.

"You'd be surprised how many people use that," Rogers said. "You can't really get a cell phone signal out here."

The Lake City Methodist Church still has services and serves as a meeting place, Rogers said.

Yet, one of the only businesses that remain these days includes a part-time concert yard/art business operated by Kenton Ray in front of the abandoned school. Ray, who works at the gypsum mill in Medicine Lodge, hopes to expand the business once he retires in a few years.

A seasonal elevator also is still running, but only during harvests, Hoagland said.

The elevator sits next to abandoned ghost tracks, complete with railroad crossing signs. The last train went through in the 1990s, Rogers said.

"It was Memorial Day weekend," Rogers said. "We were having our annual alumni dinner and the last train went through and tooted its horn on a Sunday."

She paused for a moment, and then added that it was sad to see these little towns go and folks move away. However, she couldn't imagine living anywhere else.

She and her husband, Grant, moved into the old Lake homestead in the mid-1990s upon retirement.

"We could have lived any place we wanted to," she said. "We wanted to live here in spite of the drought, the wind and the heat in the summer and the cold in the winter."

Photos by Amy Bickel/The Hutchinson News

A sink still hangs on the wall of the second floor of an old building in Lake City.

Above: Gas pumps sit in a line in front of the abandoned fuel stop in Lake City, a Barber County town that rests amid the scenic Gypsum Hills.

Left: A pay phone in Lake City still has a dial tone.

Aetna

❖ Barber County ❖

This Gyp Hills town now is part of media tycoon Ted Turner's ranch

Bleached white from the sun, the buffalo skulls rest on the fence of the old cemetery here that is marked with just a few dozen gravestones.

A trail leads to the nearly forgotten cemetery, hidden in a valley near the abandoned town site.

And, not far in the distance, hundreds, if not thousands, of media tycoon Ted Turner's bison graze on windswept pastures amid the Gyp Hills – the only living inhabitants of this former cowboy town.

Not that Aetna was ever really big. But for residents around it, the Barber County hamlet was the closest community within 30 miles in the days of horses. It had a school, a post office and a few businesses.

Aetna was rustic, a rough sort of town, recalls 87-year-old Vergie Reed, who lived in the area with her husband, Dewey, for 50 years. Dewey was once a hired man and manager of the Z-Bar Ranch, the land Turner now owns.

Vergie Reed said there was a store where a wisp of a woman with the toughest backbone around ran the counter and cut meat.

"She was mean – she had a long meat cutter and she'd get to talking and chop that down on the block," she recalled with a chuckle. "She was a pretty rough old woman."

There also was a barn where dances were held – parties that sometimes got a little on the rowdy side, Reed said.

"We hadn't been married long when we went to watch the barn dance," Reed said, noting she and Dewey have been married 70 years. "A fight got started out front, and I told Dewey, 'Let's go home,' and we never went back."

But these days, nothing is left but the cemetery, a few dilapidated structures and the buffalo. Aetna sits on Aetna Road in a sparsely populated part of Barber County – where typically the only people traveling it are cowboys in farm trucks.

Sometimes Eva Yearout, who helps her husband, Keith, manage Turner's ranch, will see a few visitors searching for the cemetery where their relatives are buried.

There was a time when Aetna had considerable pretensions. Like many a Kansas ghost town, founders wanted the city to be a commercial center. Nevertheless, according to one historical article in the March 2, 1900, Medicine Lodge Cresset, "where it was proposed to have a public park is now a horse pasture and on the site reserved for manufacturers the gentle cow chews her cud in contentment."

Or buffalo, as is the case today.

Aetna formed around 1885. According to the Aetna Clarion's Sept. 3, 1885, edition, the town was in the best area of the state.

It read as follows:

Aetna! The Queen of the West! Grow rich with the Country. Invest while you can! Aetna is situated upon a beautiful eminence in Southwestern Barber County, two miles east of the Comanche County line and six miles north of the Indian Territory line.

Surrounding the town are the large and fertile valleys of Salt Fork River, Big Mule creek, Ash creek, Dry creek, Cottage creek, Sand creek, Yellowstone creek, and others too numerous to mention, all of which have large groves of timber along their courses. Aetna is 30 miles west of New Kiowa – the nearest town of any consequence – also 35 miles southwest of Medicine Lodge, the county seat of Barber County. Aetna is also on the surveys of the Southern Kansas and the Fort Scott & Wichita Railways, and at their proposed crossing. A stage line from New Kiowa to Englewood, Clark County, via Aetna, has been located and will soon be in operation.

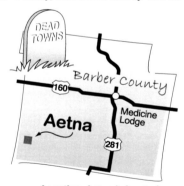

Location: Aetna is located near the intersection of Cottage Creek Road and Aetna Road in the southwest corner of Barber County. The Aetna Cemetery is just a few miles east on Cottage Creek Road.

Yet, while the town didn't fulfill its prophecies, it was a gathering point for residents, said 91-year old Mike Platt. His grandparents are buried in the Aetna cemetery. He recalls riding a horse to the Aetna school – a one-room structure that for years held students from first through eighth grades.

"Us kids always rode our horses to school and, when school was out, we went to Aetna and made ourselves a sandwich and then would go home," Platt said.

Aetna

Bison roam the open rangeland near the ghost town of Aetna.

"It had a half-dozen homes," he said of the time he was growing up.

"But it was away bigger town before I was even born. There was a hotel that my dad remembers and stayed in. There was a café."

It also is in the hearts of Dewey and Vergie Reed.

For 50 years, Dewey Reed, 90, helped tend to the Z-Bar Ranch. For 50 years, he and Vergie lived near Aetna, where they raised three children who attended the Aetna school.

Vergie said money was tight, but they went shopping at the Aetna store every Saturday, which, despite the higher prices, was cheaper than driving 35 miles to Medicine Lodge or 30 miles to Hartner. At the store, they would visit with their neighbors who also were frequenting the establishment.

"That's how we'd spend our Saturday evenings," she said.

Dewey Reed said he retired in the late 1980s. The couple have lived in Kiowa ever since.

Vergie Reed said she and her husband still take drives to Aetna occasionally, although it's a bittersweet trip.

"I'll never be a town woman," she said. "That out there is home to me."

A bison skull dries in the sun in the Aetna cemetery in Barber County.

Black Wolf

❖ Ellsworth County ❖

Grain elevator, two homes, are the last structures in Black Wolf.

There once was a sign not far from the tracks that marked his little town's ambitions.

"Black Wolf, Population 45. Speed Limit 101. Watch us grow. Air and water free."

However, standing on a dirt road not far from where a few pioneer graves rest, Gene Macek watched as an afternoon train slowly chugged through Black Wolf. The sign rotted off the post several years back, he said. The store where his father would bring him to buy candy corn and salted peanuts burned down more than a decade ago. And the old barn that once drew hundreds to town for barn dances was moved to a farm around the same time.

A grain elevator, two homes and the train, "that's about all we have anymore," Macek said.

Little remains of the town Macek's great-grandparents first settled near in the 1870s.

On the Golden Belt Highway

For more than a decade, Macek, 86, a retired Ellsworth County farmer, has delved through old books and newspapers at the library, writing down the history of the town where he grew up. He's uncovered enough information to fill several binders and boxes.

Macek talks about Black Wolf with a passion, saying his ancestors came to the area in the late 1870s. He still lives on a farm not far from town.

He recalled that every Saturday his parents would sell dozens of eggs and 10 gallons of cream to the Black Wolf store. His mother even saved up enough money from the profits one winter that she purchased a new living room set. Looking back at the history, he said it's hard to imagine that a town with such commerce and activity could just disappear.

"There were under 100 people at one time," he said, adding that its location on the Golden Belt Highway made it a good pit stop.

Another sign in town once touted it as a halfway point between San Francisco and New York, complete with mileage, said Alex Vodraska, a local farmer whose family owns part of Black Wolf today.

Author Robert Day mentioned the town in his book, "The Last Cattle Drive."

No one knows for sure how Black Wolf was named, Vodraska said. Some say residents named it after an Indian chief who died in the area. Others say pioneers spotted a couple of black wolves near the site. The Black Wolf Creek does run into the Smoky Hill River from the south, a short distance east of the river bridge.

Unlike some towns that hope for a railroad, the tracks were already laid when Black Wolf formed.

In 1879, area farmers built a grain elevator near the railway and the government established a post office. Not long later, a wealthy man named Albert Jung staked a claim near Black Wolf. Jung didn't take kindly to farming, so he established a trading post.

The town, however, couldn't grow under Jung, who wouldn't sell the land. When he died, his brother, Phillip, and Phillip's son, Arthur, inherited the land and the town began to prosper.

Phillip Jung built a hotel and general store. There also was a barn for selling farm equipment. Another hotel, the Wisconsin House, rented rooms and served food.

Black Wolf continued to grow into the 20th century. In later years, there were a few more stores, two lumberyards, three elevators, a blacksmith shop, a creamery and a school. The town also had a stockyard for shipping cattle.

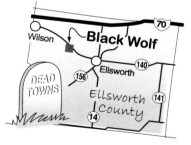

Location: Half mile south of 140 Highway near the intersection of Avenue I. Or about six miles west of Ellsworth.

In 1919, John Brickacek decided his town needed a bank, which he and other citizens promptly built. In the late 1920s, two masked men held up the bank, according to a Hutchinson News article in 1927. The bandits escaped with $500 in cash.

Another story in The News indicates law enforcement officers were pursuing the robbers a few years later.

There were floods a time or two, Macek said, showing old newspaper photos of water from the nearby Smoky Hill River surrounding businesses.

There was entertainment, too, he said. Through his research, Macek found there were as many as five saloons in

Black Wolf

Black Wolf but no shootings.

Meanwhile, two outside dance floors accommodated folks in the early part of the century. There also was the large barn that drew residents from around the county. A $1 admission was charged.

There were several baseball teams from 1895 through the 1930s. Residents even constructed a swimming pool in 1922. However, Macek, born in 1924, said it didn't last long enough for him to swim in it.

Little remains

Tall weeds grow around the foundation of the general store, which burned down in 1997. The lumberyard fell down and the blacksmith shop burned as well, said Vodraska.

The bank and depot closed in the 1950s. The post office closed in 1953.

Two houses still stand, but only one is occupied.

Trucks kick up dust on the country roads leading here – mainly during the harvest seasons. The elevator still stands, after all – the last business in Black Wolf.

There is the train – its track winding through Black Wolf on its way to either Wilson or Ellsworth. There also is the abandoned cemetery amid pasture grass. Vodraska said only a single grave marker is left.

Ghost town hunters sometimes would stop and tour the old buildings, Vodraska said. However, there is not much activity in Black Wolf these days, the two homes and the elevator really all that remains.

The latest building to vanish was the bank, which closed in 1955. Vodraska said he told a man who wanted the safe for his wife that he could have it if he would get rid of the building.

Hutchinson resident Randall Hendricks took up the challenge, said his wife, Terry. For several days, Hendricks and a few friends worked at the site. They used a car hauler and a heavy-duty winch to remove the heavy safe, which was delivered for Terry's birthday about a decade ago. Randall died five years ago, she said, but noted she still has the safe, which needs to be restored.

"That would make it hard for me to sell it at this point," she said of the sentimental value.

Ellsworth banker Curt Glaser and his family purchased the old barn. They renovated it about 10 years ago. Glaser said the hardwood dance floor is still upstairs, as well as a ticket booth and a piano, which Glaser admitted has seen better days.

His family uses the barn as a barn – putting hay upstairs and 4-H animals downstairs. They've even had a few dances, he said.

Meanwhile, the Ellsworth County Museum has the Black Wolf School, Macek said.

Looking around his town on a cold January day, Macek said Black Wolf has met the same fate as many towns that dot the Kansas landscape – towns that dwindled as people began to drive to bigger cities for groceries and as schools consolidated.

"Some of these towns are going downhill," he said. "Even Wilson has dwindled. Kids go to college and don't come back."

❖❖❖

This Ellsworth County Independent Reporter shows a view of downtown Black Wolf around the turn of the 20th century. The paper was published in 2001.

Carneiro

❖ Ellsworth County ❖

No longer a sheep shipping point, church still opens its doors each Sunday.

The bells of the steeple chime in parishioners every Sunday morning at the little white church in this rural Kansas town.

And it seems, it doesn't matter that the school closed years ago or that fewer than a half-dozen residents live here. Pastor Steve Holmes continues to bring a message to his 20 some-member Carneiro United Methodist Church congregation each Sunday – just as other ministers did for 125 years.

"Kansas, like the commercials say, gives you a sense of wide-open spaces," he said, noting that this ghost town of sorts "doesn't have the hustle and bustle of the city.

"I just think it's closer to God that way," he said.

Take a drive through the Smoky Hills past Kanopolis Reservoir and the Ellsworth County town of Carneiro suddenly appears amid the sloping terrain along Kansas Highway 140. These days, all that's left of the once-prosperous sheep shipping point are a few homes, the boarded-up school, a dilapidated general store and the well-manicured church.

Yet, the little town still has a pulse thanks, in part, to the weekly church services, as well as a monthly community potluck in the church's small addition. The town is also a tourist stop for those visiting Kanopolis Reservoir and recent local lore suggests the area might have buried treasure connected to the notorious outlaw Jesse James.

Additionally, an investor is offering home lots just east of town, which, says area resident and farmer Jon Sneath with a laugh, would surely double or triple the town's population if there were any takers.

However, a few years after the initial announcement, nothing has been built.

"Our population would probably double really quick if just one home was built," he said.

Small town, big dreams

Early founders had lofty dreams for this little waypoint along a westward path.

Before its official naming, Carneiro started as a site where the Smoky Hill Trail crossed Alum Creek, according to the U.S. Corps of Engineers. It was called the Alum Creek Station.

In 1866, the Kansas City and Santa Fe Stage and Mail Line began to travel the military trail from Kansas City to Denver. Local historian and Kansas Cowboy newspaper founder Jim Gray of Geneseo tells the story of how five soldiers were escorting a stage from Salina to Ellsworth. Though told to save their ammo, the men took "pot shots" at buffalo along the way.

"They were attacked by Indians," Gray said. "The soldiers stopped by the (Alum) Creek bank to hold off the Indians, and they started running out of ammunition. Only one made it to Ellsworth alive."

The stage stop, however, didn't really prosper until E.W. Wellington came to Kansas in the 1870s. Massachusetts- born Wellington, a Harvard graduate, brought his new wife, Clara, as well as his Harvard friends and associates from Boston to Kansas, where he eventually began an extensive sheep operation in Ellsworth County. He called his ranch Monte Carneiro, Carneiro meaning sheepfold in Portuguese.

He built many houses and ranches to accommodate himself, friends and workers, Gray said. With the large amount of sheep, Wellington, whose ranch was a few miles north of present-day Carneiro, and his group decided to develop a shipping point for the livestock in 1882, which is how the town sprang up.

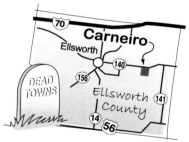

Location: On 140 Highway about nine miles east of Ellsworth.

Businesses included a hotel, stockyards, a school and three general stores, Sneath said. According to the Kansas State Historical Society, the post office was started in June 1882. Holmes said his little church began in 1885 in a school building, which was eventually razed to make way for the "new" school built in 1916. The Methodists used the basement for services, while the Christian Church used the upstairs.

In the mid-1890s, producer Henry McManes said he would help build the new church, providing two lots and the services of his hired hands. The white church's first service was in March 1895. Residents built the school in 1916 – the same year that Wellington decided to get out of the sheep business.

Wellington, who also had interests in Ellsworth, including the development of an entire city block, reported to an Ellsworth newspaper that he was selling his herd due to low tariff on wool. The article said he was contemplating turning the 19,000-acre ranch into an immense sugar plantation.

Shell of itself

There are no sugar plantations or sheep farms across the Ellsworth County prairie these days. Instead, wheat fields and cattle have taken over the former sheep center, 67-year-old Sneath said.

The stockyards are all gone where residents loaded up cattle and sheep on trains. The old school, however, remains, perched atop a small knoll – cracked and weedy concrete steps leading up to brick structure.

The old general store still stands on Carneiro's main drag. Local farmer Jon Sneath estimates that the last business in it, an antique/junk shop, closed in the 1990s.

Photos by Amy Bickel/The Hutchinson News

Still full of activity

While a shell of its former self, Holmes says that on certain days, activity still bustles in little Carniero.

The Methodist church's monthly potlucks draw nearly 50 to town for community fellowship on the third Sunday of each month, Holmes said.

Other activity also keeps tiny Carneiro on the map. Gray included Carneiro on the Kanopolis Lake Legacy Trail he developed several years ago, which highlights different historical points around the reservoir.

Meanwhile, Michelle Vanek, a transplant who married local Albert Vanek, writes a column for the Ellsworth Independent-Reporter called "The Carneiro Café." And, Sneath says, there's a couple of people, including Wichitan Ron Pastore, searching in the area for "Jesse James' Hidden Treasure" The are digging around areas of Kansas as part of a History Channel documentary.

Turns out, in Pastore's opinion, anyway, that James might not have died, instead living to a ripe old age and hiding his loot before his death, Sneath said. Moreover, James may have had a sister who lived near Carneiro.

"They're finding a few things," he said, adding that the whole theory, he guesses, "is a possibility."

As for Holmes, he has no plans to quit preaching at the little white church anytime soon, nor at the Methodist church where he also ministers in nearby Kanopolis.

"It's personal and personable both," he said. "It's more intimate, if you know what I mean. We as humans want to have great big things. However, there are smaller things that are a little more meaningful."

Sneath said the high school closed in the early 1940s with the building staying open as a grade school for at least another 20 years.

"There were 17 in the entire grade school," Sneath said of his time at Carneiro's elementary in the 1950s, adding that by eighth grade, he had just three in his class.

Sneath graduated from Ellsworth High school in 1961,went to Kansas State University and then enlisted into the Air Force for five years before coming back to the family farm at Carneiro.

This is his home, after all, he said. It's where one of his great-grandfathers first homesteaded. Another ran a feed store. One of the general stores still stands, complete with old display cases, collections and junk filling the inside, but Sneath wasn't sure if it was the one his ancestor operated.

Sneath's old home sits in what he calls "the suburbs." A few homes in town are inhabited, but most are abandoned – including what some say once was Wellington's estate, located next to the school.

Less than a half dozen, Sneath reckons, actually live in the city limits.

Old cars are over grown with weeds near a home on the outskirts of Carneiro.

Mitchell

❖ Rice County ❖

Actress Shirley Knight grew up in Mitchell.

Standing by the old Mitchell school, Rice County farmer Delmer Conner recalls when children filled the playground and took part in a game of baseball beneath the diamond lights.

Yet, nearly 60 years have passed, and Conner can only shake his head in dismay.

"It's sad," he said as he glanced around the former schoolyard where just the frame of a swing set and a rusted merry-go-round remain – not far from the former ball field now covered in waist-high weeds.

He grew up near this town, he said. Conner was a Kansas farm boy who recalls, during the 1940s, coming with his father once a week to the local elevator and purchasing a 5-cent soda.

But life has changed since those years. When the school closed, people left. Now the town's population is living in just a handful of houses.

"When they consolidated the schools, when the school closed, that is when Mitchell, our community, died," he said.

The Mitchell post office opened in 1882, according to the Kansas State Historical Society. At one time, there was a grocery store, a hardware store, a lumberyard, a coal bin and a depot. Houses dotted several blocks and, Conner estimates, at one time, 120 people lived in Mitchell during its heyday.

"There even was someone who manufactured breakfast food," Conner said of a company that operated during the 1930s and early 1950s. "They popped popcorn and sold it for breakfast cereal.

"Back then, it was still a viable little town," he said.

Early settlers included W.H. Rife, who first settled on Cow Creek in 1870. Even Conner's family homesteaded in the area, although Conner said he isn't sure how the town was named Mitchell.

Mitchell had a doctor for a time, Flavius Smith, who started practicing there in 1889, according to the Standard History of Kansas and Kansans. Mitchell also received type in a Chicago newspaper in January 1898 when Adolph Campbell, of Mitchell, "attempted to drown himself at the foot of Dock Street yesterday."

Mitchell did have a famous daughter. Actress Shirley Knight grew up in Mitchell, graduating from the eighth grade in 1950 with Conner, he said. She has starred in several movies, including "Endless Love," "As Good as It Gets" and "Divine Secrets of the Ya-Ya Sisterhood."

Conner said he wasn't born yet when the bank was operating although he had an uncle who worked as a teller there for a time. He doesn't recall the general store or the hardware store – they were all gone before he was born in 1936.

There was the elevator, however, he said. And, for a time, there was a train. He recalls his father riding the railroad's doodlebug east to get a 1940s Farmall H tractor, then driving it home. The doodlebug also hauled cream and eggs to McPherson.

Conner drove the streets on a January morning, pointing to a city block that is nothing but grass. The houses have burned, fallen down or were moved to a more prospering town, he said. A concrete bank vault still stands, the building around it crumbled years ago. An old telephone building is hidden in the trees, just a shell of its former state.

The Methodist Church closed not long after the school, Conner said. He has the cornerstone, which says it was built in 1916. Around 2010, a man had tried to renovate the church, even putting on a new roof, new doors and new windows. However, work stopped and Conner said he heard the building had been sold to someone else.

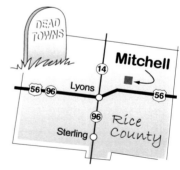

Location: Mitchell is a half-mile north of Highway 56, about 5.5 miles east of Lyons.

"It would be nice if someone could bring it back to life and make a home out of it," he said, but added he didn't know if that would happen.

The church parsonage eventually burned down, Conner said. The old cistern pump is on the property.

The depot was moved to Walton, he said. His grandson, Jeremy Showalter, uses the elevator for his farming operation. Old foundations can still be seen, as well as remnants of sidewalks.

Then there is the school. A local family owns the building, keeping it in good shape, Conner said. The town had a

Mitchell

reunion there in the past 10 years. Mitchell's school was built in 1926, the sign above the entrance reads. Peering through the windows, one can get a glimpse of a well-kept gymnasium.

The school closed in the 1960s, he said. It makes him feel for other little towns struggling to keep their schools.

"When they close the schools, little towns die," he said.

Conner went to Lyons High School and then graduated from Kansas State University in 1958.

He eventually came back to the farm where he has been ever since – raising a family near the ghost town. Now he wants to preserve Mitchell's history. He knows in a few decades what little remains of Mitchell might disappear altogether.

"It's sad to think about what it used to be," he said.

Delmer Conner, 75, said the Methodist Church in Mitchell closed shortly after the school closed. A man started to fix it up to live in the building, putting in new windows, doors and a roof. Work has stopped, however, and Conner doesn't know if his former place of worship will be renovated.

Amy Bickel/The Hutchinson News

Wherry

❖ Rice County ❖

In 1967, what remained of Wherry went up in smoke

Growing up in the 1960s, Jim Arwood watched as this ghost town disappeared completely, not only from its location off a rural country road in Rice County, but also from the map and most people's memory.

The remnants of Wherry, Kansas, are marked only by an overgrown railroad bed and maybe a few chunks of concrete, along with a clump of cottonwood trees.

"It seems over the years that between our visits a little bit of the town would disappear – torn down or burned down – I don't exactly recall the reasons," Arwood said, noting his mother would sometimes stop at the abandoned ghost town on the way from Lyons to visit his grandparents in Hutchinson.

In February 1967, what remained of Wherry went up in smoke.

This is the story of a town that grew and then died in less than 40 years.

Wherry is a town that, after death, maybe became even more popular as a place to explore – including by youth on Halloween night. These days, the traffic passing Wherry are just farmers traipsing back in forth in their pickups to farm fields. And only a few old-timers can recall the town whose heyday peaked in the 1910's before it began to dwindle to nothingness.

A town with a dream

The railroad town started as a post office on April 17, 1888, closing, ironically, on Halloween of 1923, according to the Kansas State Historical Society.

It once had a store, a hotel, lumberyard, railroad station, grain elevators and houses. In fact, at one time, the town and its vicinity had 300 people, said Gary Battey, who was helping cut soybeans just a few miles north of Wherry's location.

He remembers an old house that he once ventured into – maybe the hotel. The inside had a Wild West look with its balcony – just the type used as backdrops in the old western movies.

According to Daniel Fitzgerald, the author of several Kansas ghost town books, it's not clear why Wherry was called Wherry. Most of the buildings were built between 1910 and 1915, as the town boomed with the location next to the railroad.

Joe and Al Hauschild built the lumberyard, hardware and machinery store. Farmers would travel to town to visit with

Jonas Neun.

Another popular spot was the home of Steve Thompson, the first person in town to own a phonograph. He would bring the machine outside and folks would set up chairs to listen to the music.

Wherry's prosperity began to decline in the 1920s, however. The general store and post office closed and residents began to travel to bigger cities for goods. The final demise came during two separate events in February 1967,when, according to The Hutchinson News, the general store, followed by an old Hauschild home, were destroyed by fire, "blamed on trysting neckers who perhaps were careless while smoking."

Joe Hedrick, Nickerson, who owns part of the section that butts up to the old town site, said little, if anything remains. Maybe a few concrete pieces, he said – if the remains haven't been buried by dirt work.

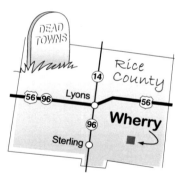

Location: Wherry is located about six miles north of Nickerson on 23rd Road in Rice County, between roads U and T on the east side of the road.

Childhood memories

Yet for Jim Arwood and his sister, Sally Beydler, the name Wherry brings about fond childhood memories.

Beydler, who lives in Hutchinson, said their mother, Jenny Arwood, now in her 90s, recalls square dancing on a roof in the town in the 1930s. Jenny Arwood was the adventurous type and loved to take her children on a journey during their weekly trips to Hutchinson.

Arwood said he remembers the hotel the most – a two-story building that he loved because it looked like something out of the television show "Gunsmoke."

"I also remember the bank and there were several other abandoned homes," he said.

The youngest of five children, he was a bit scared of going inside but would watch his mother, along with his four sisters, disappear through the doorways of the worn-down structures.

Wherry

"I was sure there were ghosts on the inside," he said.

Arwood, who now lives in Phoenix, said he visits Kansas a couple times a year, taking his own family to the stops that were a large part of his past.

"It is definitely a fond memory from my childhood," Arwood said. "It is amazing that something as simple as an old abandoned building … could have been the highlight of a journey.

"But I guess during those days, kids were more interested in their surroundings. We didn't have iPods to keep us entertained. Instead of asking 'are we there yet?' We wanted to stop and see something."

From The Hutchinson News, March 9, 1967

Where, Oh Where, Has Wherry Went?
By Alvin Dumler

The mite on the map of Southeast Rice County's West Washington Township went the way of Carter Spur – its one-time neighbor to the southeast that sat for years at the point on Plum Street road six miles north of here where Reno-Rice-McPherson corners integrate.

Two fires, one Feb. 12 and the other Feb. 26 wiped out last vestige of the village on the Frisco railroad that was Wherry.

The building which once was the general store went first and then the big house owned by Al Hauschild of Hutchinson burned but neither figured in our Sand Hills prairie fires.

Built In 1910
Hutchinson's Al Hauschild and his father, Joe, built the house in 1910. Hauschild owns the farm eight miles east and a mile north of Sterling.

Both Carter Spur and Matheson have faded. In the days of Sand Hill bootleggers and national prohibition four decades ago, Carter Spur had its moment of glory as our Wicked border town, sitting where three counties met.

Wherry had a store, lumber yard, railroad station, post office.

It was more "metropolitan" even than "the Tri-Co. Spur." Sand Hills stockmen used Matheson as a cattle loading point.

These fires were not related in any way to the big prairie grass holocausts of last week but were blamed on trysting neckers who perhaps were careless while smoking.

Between Buhler and Saxman, the Frisco has only Medora nestling alongside it to break the monotony for the crew of the occasional freight train.

The clump of trees in the distance at the end of n old railroad bed is the location of the town of Wherry.

Carter Spur

❖ Rice County ❖

Residents recall activities during 1930s Prohibition at the notorious little store at Carter Spur

History, it seems, wants to forget about the wicked little Rice County stop of Carter Spur.

It's been decades since the spot on the intersection where Rice, Reno and McPherson counties meet on Plum Street has been on a map. The Kansas State Historical Society doesn't mention it on its list of more than 5,000 dead towns, although Carter Spur was much livelier than some communities that have met the same fate.

Only a few old-timers recall the name and most only recall a few bits and pieces of what happened here. In addition, the only thing that is left of Carter Spur, something that marks the place of wild parties, of drunkenness, gambling and bootlegging, is a small piece of concrete slab next to the abandoned Frisco railway.

No one knows how the stop got started, how it met its final demise or even how it got the name of Carter, although an early 1940s story in The News recorded a Carter family living near Carter Spur.

It may have first been formed by the railroad, said Arlen Lindquist, who lives closer to Windom, a McPherson County town about 15 miles to the north.

Kenny Knight, who owns Knight Feedlot near Lyons, said he has a county plat map from 1919 that shows Carter Spur having two elevators. And a News story from 1927 said Lyons Flour Milling Co., of Lyons, had elevators in the now ghost towns of Pollard, Saxman, Wherry and Carter Spur, as well as the existing town of Chase.

But those who still remember some details about Carter Spur don't know it for milling or even for the railroad. They know it for a store that sold gasoline and some grocery items like bread, milk and oil for kerosene lamps. They know it had a backroom where drinking and gambling took place, as well as dances.

"My dad would have skinned my hide if I would have went back there," said Hutchinson resident Vic Willems who remembers riding his horse in his early teen years to Carter Spur most Sundays in the late 1930s and early '40s to watch area residents practice their skills at roping and bull riding.

"They sold groceries, they had gas later on and then there was the backroom where they played cards," he said.

A notorious place

The store, however, was a little more notorious than just a little whiskey and card playing. There were fights and even a few murders.

In May 1924, a man named Verne Wagoner, an "alleged Reno County rum runner," shot and killed Pearl Kelly, whom The News back then described as a "Kansas City underworld character."

Wagoner claimed Kelly and two associates attempted to hold up a craps game. The state sought to prove Wagoner shot Kelly in a quarrel growing out of the craps game.

Area rancher Menno Enns said he remembers being part of a group on horseback in search of a body sometime in the late 1930s.

He remembers the group found a shallow grave and alerted authorities.

Enns, who was 88 in 2011, said his parents would stop at the store for some groceries as well as fuel. He, too, rode his horse to the rodeos, organized by local farmer Claude Borders.

In 1938, after the place was busted, Rice County Sheriff Claude Suttle said he found seven pints of whiskey and alcohol in the cars and a large number of empty liquor cartons.

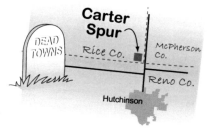

Location: At the intersection of Plum and 108th Avenue on the northwest corner in Rice County.

"Something will have to be done," Suttle said. "That place is causing too much trouble."

Yet no one is sure when the little store closed or who even ran it.

And then it disappeared

Edith Enns, Menno's wife, said she remembers going into the store when the two were dating, maybe about 1942. She remembered seeing a picture of a woman painted on the front-room floor, which Menno called "the face on the barroom floor."

Carter Spur

The two married and moved away while Menno served in World War II. They returned in 1946 and neither remembers the store there at that time.

Jane Nickel, who moved with her husband from California to a home about 2 miles from Carter Spur, recalls taking the "Doodlebug" from Carter Spur to Medford, Oklahoma, with her 1-year-old son. The store building was there at the time, she recalls, but it wasn't open.

And Willems, who worked shortly after high school along the Frisco line that went through Carter Spur, as well as Medora, Buhler and Burrton, said he didn't remember the store still standing at that time.

Menno said that eventually a man named Bill Blessing sold the site of Carter Spur to Hutchinson Dr. John Blank. Blank's wife had a big garden and sold vegetables, as well as cider, from a stand across the road.

The land is still in the family. Sharon Blank lives just a

Menno and Edith Enns sit at their kitchen table talking about an old railroad stop called Carter Spur.

few hundred yards from the old Carter Spur site. She said there is a small piece of concrete, along with metal, among the trees where the store sat.

She said she moved to the area in the 1960s, marrying Dr. Blank's son, Don. She has heard the stories that her corner was a party spot.

She recalled a train going by once a day with just a few cars. The railroad eventually tore out the track, she said, estimating that happened at least 20 years ago.

The last mention of Carter Spur in The News was in 1967, by Alvin Dumler, who wrote a column called "The High Plains."

"Both Carter Spur and (nearby) Matheson have faded," he penned. "In the days of Sand Hill bootleggers and national prohibition four decades ago, Carter Spur had its moment of glory as our wicked border town, sitting where the three counties met."

From The Hutchinson News, Sept. 19, 1938

Two Containing Booze Seized In Spur Raid

Two automobiles seized when officers of three counties paid an unexpected visit to a combination grocery store, beer parlor and dance hall at Carter Spur early Sunday morning were still unclaimed in custody of Sheriff Claude Suttle of Rice County at Lyons today.

One car, a 1931 Ford roadster, carries Sedgwick county tags, while the other, a Chevrolet coupe, was licensed in Reno County. The officers said they found seven pints of whiskey and alcohol in the cars and a large number of empty liquor cartons.

Officers of Reno, Rice and McPherson counties met and went to the place in a group at 1:30 a.m. Sunday morning, "shaking down" cars and frequenters. They said about 50 persons were at the nightspot. No arrests were made.

The drink-dance place, north of Hutchinson on the Plum road, is in Rice County but is with stone's toss of Reno and McPherson counties. Sheriff George T. Allison of Reno said he has received complaints of drunkenness from the vicinity.

Sheriff Suttle planned to confer with the Rice County attorney as to possible action.

"Something will have to be done," Suttle said. "That place is causing too much trouble."

The ghost town Carter Spur was in the northwest corner of the intersection of Plum Street and Avenue Y where Rice County, McPherson County and Reno County meet.

Reno Center

❖ Reno County ❖

"I expect to see the day that Reno Center will not only be a bigger town than Hutchinson, but also the county seat."
Reno Center resident Tom Crotts, however, was wrong.

Folks in this little settlement had high hopes it would be the Reno County seat.

The location was prime – the center of Reno County. It already was on a freight trail and there seemed to be plans by the railroad for a line to run through the hamlet.

"I expect to live to see the day that Reno Center will not only be a larger town than Hutchinson, but also the county seat," local resident and proponent Tom Crotts told a newspaperman in the 1870s.

Fast-forward 140 years and it's evident Crotts was wrong. Hutchinson is, by far, the biggest city in the county and it has the courthouse, to boot. Meanwhile, Reno Center isn't even a dot on a map, the location just a no-till field south of the tiny town of Partridge, said area resident Jim French.

This, however, is more than a story of a Kansas ghost town. It's about Hutchinson's beginnings, of wheeling and dealing, of how the Santa Fe Railroad steamed into Partridge in 1886 and Reno Center was history.

Starting a town

Long before there was a town, there was a freight trail. Dubbed the Sun City Trail, it was used by freighters who hauled supplies to Barber County's Sun City where the U.S. Army had built a stockade to hold unruly Indians caught outside their assigned area, according to the book "Legend and Legacy, Partridge Kansas 1886-1986," by Naomi Stiggins.

Chris Terrill, a local historian and teacher, said most who settled the area were Civil War veterans restless to get out of their hometowns.

Among the residents were the Rev. Samuel Dilley and his family, including son Zenas and daughter and son-in-law Durilla and H.C. O'Hara, who staked claims in the area a mile south of Partridge in 1872, Terrill said.

Stiggins' book says Reno Center received a post office in December 1873. A few weeks earlier the First Church of Christ was organized, meeting in Zenas Dilley's home.

At the time, it was just the county's second church, Terrill said.

The Rev. Dilley donated the land for the church, school and cemetery. Dreams were that Reno Center would grow bigger, becoming the county's commercial center, Terrill said. A man with an agenda, however, fouled the plan.

His name was C.C. Hutchinson.

First attempt and a notch

Hutchinson, founder of the town that bears his name, realized his town could lose the contest for the county seat. Thus, he got himself appointed as a representative in the state Legislature and went to Topeka with one goal in mind – to ensure Hutchinson got the title.

To become a county seat, a town needed to be located near the center of its county and to have a somewhat substantial population. County seats were places of commerce, after all, and needed to be central enough so residents could travel to town, do their business and make it home in one day.

When the Legislature first formed Reno and Rice counties, the northern tier of townships in Reno County were designated as a part of Rice and McPherson counties. This put Hutchinson, though the biggest town in the county by far, just a few miles from the northern border – and ineligible to be a county seat.

Hutchinson, however, decided it was time to redraw the map, gaining help from Rice County Rep. F.J. Griffith, according to a story in The News. In Rice County, the largest town was Peace, which later became Sterling. However, a substantial number of people lived in the northern part of the county, near present-day Lyons, and they hoped to secure the seat for themselves.

With Griffith's help, Hutchinson convinced the Legislature to pass a bill that took five townships away from Rice County and two away from McPherson County to extend Reno County's northern border to its present- day location. As part of the deal, legislators cut off the northern end of Harper County and a row of townships from the south of Reno, which helped form Kingman County.

"This made Hutchinson more nearly in the center of the

Location: North of the intersection of Longview Road and Partridge Road on the east side.

county and Reno Center's hopes of becoming the county seat were dashed," wrote Stiggins. The swap paid off for Griffith, too. In 1876, the people of Rice County voted against making Peace the county seat and decided to build a new town that would receive the designation – Lyons.

Still, residents of southern Rice County, feeling short changed, wanted a bridge over the Arkansas River to promote traffic traveling from the south. Reno County, not wanting to pay the expense of building and maintaining a bridge so far from a town, decided to come up with a compromise: Four square-mile sections of land would be given back to Rice County if the county agreed to build and maintain a bridge, The News reported. Both counties agreed and the current "notched" border exists to this day.

A second death

While little Reno Center missed its first chance at taking the title, residents here weren't giving up, despite the death of early founder Zenas Dilley.

Dilley was struck by lightning while bringing his stud from Hutchinson back to Reno Center. While his family attempted an old Indian remedy, bathing him in mud up to his neck, Zenas died a few days later, Terrill said.

In 1885, a tornado damaged part of the first settlement of Reno Center, Stiggins reported. With the land one mile north already marked off by the Santa Fe Railroad, some people chose to relocate closer to this main line.

Still, townspeople had another glimpse of possibly securing the county seat. Some Wichitans had a plan to bring a railroad through Reno Center – a new Wichita-to Colorado line that would go from Sedgwick County to Kinsley.

Backers received a charter on July 27, 1885. However, a railroad strike and the ingenuity of a Hutchinson politician, an editor and a half-dozen promoters brought the Missouri Pacific to Hutchinson and kept Wichita "from being the exclusive capital of south-central Kansas as Sedgwick County boosters had schemed."

"The story of how the Missouri Pacific came to town is one of our more fascinating chapters," a News editor reported in a December 1973 column.

Realizing their town's potential fate, four Hutchinson men went to New York to persuade Missouri Pacific Railroad mag-

nate Jay Gould to build a railroad through Hutchinson. At the time, Gould was amid a brutal railroad strike. His stations at Atchison and Parsons had been burned, and he was looking at bypassing the state of Kansas all together. However, he told the delegates, if they could assure him they would protect his property, they would likely get whatever they wanted, Stiggins wrote.

The delegates enlisted the help of Hutchinson News Editor Ralph Easley, who alarmed politicians in western Kansas to meet in Topeka to help Gov. Martin end the strike so the rail would be built, according to The News. The politicians came. Martin got the message. Easley wrote a proclamation threatening to call the militia if the strikers persisted. The governor signed it and the strike stopped.

And Reno Center's dream of being the county-seat town died a second death.

Last punch

The people of Reno Center had been so sure the Santa Fe Railroad would come through, they built a depot for it, according to Hutchinson resident Bert Newton's book "Early Ghost Towns, Post Offices and Hamlets in Reno County, Kansas," published in 2004.

With the railroad moving to the north, the few who lived in Reno Center began to move the town to the tracks, Newton wrote. The depot moved in 1887 and the post office on May 24, 1886.

Locals also moved the church that year. Using logs, residents pulled it to the new site, Terrill said.

"If the Santa Fe was responsible for the death of Reno Center, it played mid wife at the birth of Partridge." Stiggins wrote.

Railroad officials named each station on the line. The station closest to Reno Center was dubbed Partridge, after a railroad official, although the name "Reno Center" was written on the bottom of a cash drawer.

Stiggins wrote that legend has it the postmaster wrote postal officials asking them to send the mail by train to Partridge station instead of by stage to Reno Center. So officials changed their books to read Partridge and would not change the name back to Reno Center, though many residents were outraged.

The name controversy continued 12 more years, Stiggins reported, but the name Partridge stuck. Even the Reno Center Cemetery donated by the Rev. Dilley became Partridge Cemetery.

In this photo students are seen attending Reno Center School. The school building was later moved into Partridge.

Reno Center's original First Church of Christ is shown after it was moved into Partridge.

Photos courtesy Chris Terrill

Castleton

❖ Reno County ❖

*The 20th Century Fox movie 'Wait 'Til the Sun Shines, Nellie,'
filmed in this once vibrant town.*

For a fleeting moment, this little town was touched by the silver screen.

It was 1951, Francie White Grilliot recalls. She and her grade-school friends were excited to be part of the background in a Hollywood motion picture shot on location in their hometown of Castleton – a film called "Wait 'Til the Sun Shines, Nellie."

The film crew transformed little Castleton into Sevillinois, Ill., a town set in 1905. They built a fire station, barbershop, livery stable and other period pieces that were situated around the already existing post office and Santa Fe depot. They kept a wardrobe of old-time clothing at the high school, and Grilliot's mother, a seamstress, was charged to make the costumes fit the extras.

For about two weeks, Castleton boomed with activity. But, then the crew packed up and headed west and the tiny town of Castleton, already well amid rural decline, continued its downward spiral.

The post office closed in 1957 and the red brick depot, which had attracted the eye of the Hollywood producer, was razed in the early 1960s.

"There's not much left," Francie said from the kitchen table in the farmhouse where she grew up.

Castleton is where her family homesteaded, including an early town resident, Anthony Smyth. She and her husband, Tom, raised seven children on the farm that Smyth once owned. A town street is named after the family.

Castleton is also where the Grilliots married in 1961, a ceremony set in a little Catholic church also demolished in the late 1990s.

A solid start

Like all towns, Castleton founders had dreams for the stagecoach stop platted by C.C. Hutchinson in 1872. Hutchinson already had founded the city of Hutchinson, which eventually would secure the county seat of Reno County. He named Castleton after his new bride's hometown in Vermont.

William Wallace built the town's first business, a general store and tavern in his residence, according to an article in The News. He also served as Castleton's postmaster.

The town grew to 450 people. It had two blacksmiths, a livery, a depot, meat market, groceries, hotel, restaurants, hardware and a creamer, the article stated.

Then came the death dealer, Charlie Hornbaker, the unofficial mayor, told The News when the post office closed.

"The auto not only ruined our town, but others," he said. "We can now go to Hutchinson in the time it took to hitch up the horses. But who'd want to go back to the horse and buggy days?"

Nellie shines for a time

By the 1950s, locals estimated only 80 people living in Castleton. Then Nellie came to town, giving a boost in population, temporarily.

The basic plot in "Wait 'Til the Sun Shines, Nellie" centers on a man who moves to a small town and sets up a barbershop, Tom Grilliot said, adding the movie has highs and lows for its characters.

It starred David Wayne, Hugh Marlowe and Jean Peters as Nellie. Peters was Howard Hughes' girlfriend at the time, and Hughes had hired a chaperone to make sure Peters didn't stray. Fresh roses from Hughes arrived at her room at the Bisonte Hotel in Hutchinson every morning, according to News Editor Stuart Awbrey's column from the 1960s.

Awbrey said he was traveling west after the Castleton filming, so he stopped in to see the director, Henry King, who was putting finishing touches on the film.

"King was using the studio's biggest sound stage, and on it was a re-creation of what had been at Castleton a few weeks before," Awbrey wrote. "The railroad station seemed to have been rebuilt, stick for stick, and rubbed to the same dilapidated look. And, of course, the barbershop, firehouse and such might have been moved directly from central Reno County.

"I was stunned," Awbrey continued to write.

Location: About 1 ½ miles west of Highway 17 between Broadacres and Valley Pride roads.

"What was that bit about getting authenticity in Kansas?" Awbrey asked King.

"Well, we salvaged some scenes from our trip," King said. "But after we saw the runs out here, we decided on some script changes. And I wasn't too happy about the lighting we got in Kansas."

Thus, how much of Nellie's release was actually filmed in Castleton is anyone's guess, it seems, although Francie Grilliot says she thinks she saw herself in the film.

Tom Grilliot said they don't own a copy but have home videos taken by his wife's uncle during the filming.

Faded dreams

Much of what is left of Castleton can be seen from the Grilliot's lane: the tall bins of the cooperative elevator, a few dozen houses and a community church. There's a dozen or two homes, as well, and a park with equipment and a memorial that was erected in the 1950s to those who served their country.

A faded sign on the two-story township building still reads "Sam Eichenbarger, General Merchandise," which, according to a 1970 story in The News, was seen in the film. The high school closed in the 1950s and the grade school a decade or so later.

In 1955, the Santa Fe ran its last Doodlebug train, and Hornbaker bought tickets so all Castleton youngsters could have the last ride to Hutchinson. The post office closed in June 1957, and in the early 1970s moved to Great Bend. It's still on display at a museum.

"Like a condemned man marking time on the wall, Castleton chalks up another loss when its weather beaten, 85-year-old post office closes its doors for the last time Friday – no longer a necessary part of the postal system," wrote News reporter Jim Banman.

"The village will mark the passing, as it did the closing of the Santa Fe depot, by digging a few scoops of loam, making a mound and placing a few flowers on it."

Much has changed from Hornbaker's day, who told The News in the late 1950s that there was a time when it was hard to find a place to park with all the horses and buggies on the street.

In the article, Hornbaker recalled a fire destroying one of the groceries and the Odd Fellow's Lodge around 1938. The lumberyard just folded and the blacksmith went out with the invention of the auto.

"I guess no one is to blame for this deterioration of our town," Hornbaker had said. "It's a combination of all these things."

Yet, a bit of life and energy continues, despite the waning population, said Paulette Shultz. She and her husband decided to move their family to Castleton in the 1970s, building a new house on the outskirts of town.

"We fell in love with the area," she said. "We wouldn't want to live anywhere else."

A poster of the movie 'Wait 'Til the Sun Shines, Nellie' is a reminder of the time 1951 that Hollywood came to Castleton to film parts of a movie about a man who moves to a small town and sets up a barbershop.

Jean Peters and Hugh Marlow, stars of the movie 'Wait 'Til the Sun Shines, Nellie,' stand in front of the depot during the filming in Castleton.

Someone from the film company makes 'buggy' tracks in the dirt road for the film 'Wait 'Til the Sun Shines, Nellie' in Castleton in August, 1951. The false buildings behind him have business names painted on them for the movie.

Punkin Center

❖ Reno County ❖

Despite its funny name, Punkin Center was a real spot in Reno County and a community center.

There are no pumpkins in Punkin Center. Never have been, says 85-year-old Anna Hill with a laugh, although she says she has considered taking a tire she painted orange, printing on it the words "Punkin Center" and putting it at the intersection of where this little neighborhood once existed.

"I thought about putting that up so people at least know where it is," she said.

There are only five other states with a Punkin Center, including Texas, which has five or six with the town name, in all. And this Reno County ghost town is the only one of the dozen or so Punkin Centers that shows up on a website dedicated to the nation's funniest named towns.

There's nothing there anymore, except for a old garage that's falling down in the middle of a pasture, and Anna and Dalton Hill's home just down the road. Nevertheless, Anna Hill, who has lived in the same house since birth, said her memories are fond of the little stop in the road she calls home.

A gathering place and night baseball

In 1871, a man named Lawson brought his family to Reno County, settling at the intersection of Haven Road and Illinois Avenue, the site of the future Punkin Center. He donated some of his land for a school, called the Lawson School. Eventually, a small general store popped up as well. Yet, for years, the small spot in the road didn't have a name.

Loel Balzer, who wrote a special article on the town for The News in 1996, reported information provided by Norman Lowe on how Punkin Center was named.

"The store was still on the corner of the old Hill farm, across the road from the old Skelton farm, and across the corner from Lawson School House. The argument was: should the place be called Hillsville, Skeltonville or Lawsonville?

"A gang of men were widening the McGuire Grade on Highway 96, four miles west of Punkin Center on the old Santa Fe Trail. One day, a car came along, loaded down with brooms. One of the boys jerked one of the brooms from the car as it went by. The boss, Archie Brown, suggested we sell the broom to the highest bidder, and he would take the proceeds down to 'Punkin Center' and buy cigars for the gang. This was done and the place was called Punkin Center from then on, and I was one of the gang."

Another version tells of a farmer who was dating the new schoolteacher. He would joke that she was dating the mayor of Punkin Center. Eventually, the name stuck.

Either way, Punkin Center became Punkin Center, Anna Hill said. There were never any dreams of it becoming a metropolis like Hutchinson, but the center provided necessities for those who didn't want to travel west into Hutchinson or east into Burrton.

In the 1920s, or maybe a little earlier, Anna Hill's husband, Dalton, recalls, a new school was built. According to Balzer's article, the first wood-frame school was moved diagonally across the intersection and turned into a grocery store and filling station. Residents built a new brick school in its place.

The store burned down in 1934, according to an article in The News at the time, but the family who ran it rebuilt it. It quickly again became a gathering place for the local farmers, Anna Hill said. That included her father, who would drop her and her siblings off for school in the family's Model T Ford. On days he wasn't busy farming, he would stop in at the store to get the latest news.

Location: A mile south of U.S. 50 on Haven Road.

According to Balzer's story, farmers also would come before school let out so they could engage in a friendly game of cards in the back of the store.

"He'd sit there and visit half a day," Anna Hill said of her father with a chuckle. "It was a visiting place for the old farmers and, after school, the kids would play around there until it was time to go home."

It's where she became acquainted with her husband, she said.

Dalton Hill was one of the many who had the opportunity to play on the town's lighted ball field in the 1930s – one of maybe the only diamonds in the state under lights at the time, Anna Hill estimates.

Punkin Center

A Delco light plant supplied electricity for night games, according to the book "Early Ghost Towns, Post Offices and Hamlets in Reno County, Kansas" by Bert Newton.

Things never got too wild, Anna Hill said.

The store was robbed once. Also, in 1941, Hutchinson resident Grace McQueen was arrested at the filling station for being in possession of 35 pints of whiskey. A Hutchinson police chief spotted the booze while he was riding around.

Vanished

These days, the area neighborhood has virtually disappeared, Anna Hill said. Punkin Center died as progress advanced.

Punkin Center is no longer even a spot on the road, although some gazetteer maps still show the community.

Balzer wrote that at the end of World War II, people began to drive to Wichita and Hutchinson for shopping. Consolidation changed the school districts and the Lawson School closed in the 1950s. The store closed later. It was purchased by a couple who moved it to West 30th Avenue in Hutchinson.

Anna Hill said she thought the building still stood but didn't know the address.

She's watched the spot that once was a community center disappear. But her memories are vivid.

"I love Punkin," she said. "We spent a lot of time there."

But, she added, "It's a lot of time under the bridge."

Just a few buildings remain in the former town of Punkin Center.

An old silo is seen through the ruins of a building near what once was Punkin Center.

Punkin Center was at the corner of Haven Road and Illinois Avenue.

Reno County

❖❖ * Darlow * Elmer * Fernie * Forsha * Huntsville * Lerado * Medora * Nonpareil * ❖❖
* Occee * Ost * Pekin * Queen City * Sego * Thomas Grove * Woodberry * Yaggy *

Like Lerado, other Reno County ghost towns vanished

A lonely wind blows the cotton from the trees that have grown up in front of Lerado's dilapidated lodge hall and opera house.

The metal awning is rusted and dented, the windows boarded and the once widely used sidewalk chipped and cracked. For those not looking, they'd never realize it was there, or that this stop in the middle of the road was ever a promising metropolis.

More than a century ago, town leaders here had dreams: of houses and business, of people. They dreamed of the railroad.

But the railroad never came.

The two-story brick structure is one of just a few remaining buildings of the Reno County town. A blackboard still graces the inside of a former school turned community center – the shuffleboard lines still stenciled in the wooden floor. The merry-go-round sits in the front lawn – the wooden seats broken.

Meanwhile, just across the road is a little white church with a bell tower, the grass knee-high except for a path that leads to the church's front steps. Remains of a couple of broken-down buildings rest in the trees.

And, in the Lerado cemetery just a half-mile away is the grave of the Peters family – a father, mother and two children who were murdered in the town in the early 1990s. Four white crosses rest next to the road at their former home site, which burned the day they died.

This is Lerado today, one of nearly 75 ghost towns across Reno County – towns where residents had big aspirations. Now the former booming cities have been almost forgotten with time.

They had names like Og and Bones Springs, Sego and Ocoee, said Hutchinson resident Bert Newton, who, in 2004, chronicled the towns in the publication "Early Ghost Towns, Post Offices and Hamlets in Reno County, Kansas."

"That's one of the things I loved – the titles of them," she said. And all of them, she added, had a story.

Dust in the wind

Most of the 75 towns that dot the Reno County landscape are just memories. Square nails or a piece of concrete might be all that is left if searchers even know where to look.

Take Fernie, a town on the old railroad line located about three miles south of Hutchinson. There once was a wind-pow-

ered elevator and grinder near the Fernie brothers' house. People from the surrounding area would bring their grain to be ground into feed for livestock.

These days, just the ghost railroad line still is visible.

Any remains of Sego aren't visible from the roadway, except for a graveyard not far off Sego Road. It had a post office from 1874 to 1905, according to the Kansas State Historical Society. There also was a school, church, general store, constable and creamery.

However, by 1910, there were only 16 people living in Sego. Now there is nothing.

Ocoee – pronounced Oh'KOH-ee, according to Newton – means place where the passionflower is found in Cherokee. It had a school. The post office ran from 1879 to 1881, according to the historical society.

The town, obviously, didn't grow or spread like passionflowers, however, Newton said.

Newton said she spent a lot of time researching Woodbury, which was in southeast Reno County, wondering if the town ever had been named Antioch after the school and cemetery. The town's post office operated from 1878 to 1887.

Meanwhile, not much, except a home, remains of Pekin, located 15 miles west of Hutchinson and five miles north of Abbyville. It was named for a suburb of Peoria, Ill., and had a population of 40 in 1910, says Newton. A post office opened in 1897 but closed in 1905.

There was a store, a creamery, an icehouse and a butcher shop, along with a town hall, church and school. Pekin even had a chief of police and its own telephone company, with nearly 300 phones in the system.

First towns

Thomas Grove was Reno County's first settlement, according to Newton.

Reno County

A merry go round sits in front of the old Lerado school. The town's founder wanted to put a college in town, but the town died when the railroad missed it.

Amy Bickel/The Hutchinson News

The John Wesley Thomas family arrived in Reno County in November 1870. They were on their way from Iowa to California by covered wagon when they stopped in the county for the winter. They named the area Thomas Grove, built a sod house and lived in it and the covered wagon.

They never left.

Others arrived a year later, including one with a herd of longhorns. They built a school in 1886 and a new school in 1956. It closed in 1960.

Meanwhile, the first post office was in Queen City, or Queen Valley.

According to the Reno County Historical Society, William Caldwell heard that the Santa Fe Railroad was going to go through where Cow Creek and the Arkansas River meet. He set up a little town with a post office. The sign on the office said "Queen City." Other references call it "Queen Valley."

He had dreams of it becoming a major metropolis. According to the 1917 publication "History of Reno County," residents agreed to haul mail without cost to the government in exchange for the establishment. It also said that in addition to his duties as postmaster, Caldwell ran an inn built of prairie sod.

Queen City never had a chance to become the Reno County seat. The post office opened in July 1871. It closed Feb. 2, 1872 – about the time Hutchinson incorporated. Meanwhile, the railroad bypassed Queen City for the future county seat.

A few remnants

Only a few of the ghost towns of the county have remains – some more than others. Medora, for instance, still has a few businesses – Polk's Market and Becker's Bunkhouse. A church and the old school still stands.

Nonpareil, also spelled Nonpariel, still has the old house that served as the post office. The post office opened as Idaville in 1875, according to the Kansas State Historical Society. Eventually the name was changed, although the post office permanently closed in 1881.

Nonpareil had a school, Newton says. When it disbanded in

1897, students went to nearby Abbyville.

Sharon Covert, who lives at the former town of Darlow, located six miles south of Hutchinson, said the town once had a blacksmith, a lumberyard, two elevators, a depot, grocery and a school.

"It was a booming little town," she said. "Now there are just a few residents."

She lives in the home where her husband's grandfather, Lloyd Jacques – an early settler – once resided. Just a few doors down is the former post office turned home.

Darlow began as Booth, according to Newton. The post office opened in 1890. In 1910, there were 75 residents. However, by 1935, the post office closed and what was left of the little town began to decline even more.

Not far away is Elmer, which still has a metal elevator and a road sign marking its presence. It's where Evert Eash has lived the past 24 years – in one of only two homes that still grace the actual town site, he said.

The post office at Elmer was called Bernal, Newton said. But the railroad called the town Elmer. The town was platted in 1875. South Hutch founder Ben Blanchard even frequented the town. He was trying to sell lots in Hutchinson and tried drilling for oil. Instead he found salt and decided to "salt his well with real oil" in an effort to develop a bustling city. He stored his supply of oil at Elmer.

Newton reported that during Prohibition some Hutchinson residents used the Elmer Station to receive liquor with whisky shipped to the town in five-gallon lots.

Lerado's storied past

Lerado has its own unique ghostly presence. Only one house is near the city limits and, on a recent afternoon, the only person frequenting the town was a cemetery sexton. It also has one of the more colorful tales.

According to a Hutchinson News article from 2009, a doctor named John Brady was optimistic for the city, which included building a women's college named after him – Brady University – once the railroad went through it. Dr. Brady and the townsfolk

Reno County

prepared for trains by building a $24,000, 100-room hotel and a brickyard operation. At one time, there was a bank, a newspaper, a school, a church, a drugstore, a meat market, a town hall, the lodge and opera house and four livery barns.

The town had everything except a railroad, and the railroad never came.

The railroad wasn't impressed with Lerado's growth, New-ton said. They wanted 51 percent of the Lerado Town Co. Brady refused and the railroad built their tracks through Turon.

People left. Some moved their buildings and homes to the new town of Turon.

Now, the former town on Pretty Prairie and Lerado roads is just another bump in the road.

❖❖❖

Reno a veritable ghost town graveyard

Reno County has nearly 75 ghost towns that dotted the landscape. Here are just a few of them reported on in the publication "Early Ghost Towns, Post Offices and Hamlets in Reno County, Kansas" by Bert Newton.

Avery (Highland Park) - Once called Highland Park, the town had a store and blacksmith shop. It also had a post office from 1885 to 1901. It was located 20 miles northwest of Hutchinson on Peace Creek.

Baxterville - It had a steam plow, mason, plasterer, shoemaker and preacher.

Bland - It had a store. The post office was in operation from 1900 to 1905. There were at least 95 people being supplied mail at one time.

Bone Springs - The town was southwest of Arlington. The post office opened in 1874 and closed in 1902, according to the historical society. There was also a school.

Buffalo - Around 1873, the town had a store, a doctor, small drugstore, livery and a post office, although the Kansas State Historical Society doesn't show a post office with the name Buffalo. There also was a wind-powered flour and grist mill and a dressmaker.

Christopher - First having Pony as a suggested name, the town's post office ran from 1882 to 1892.

Dean - The post office was established in 1881 and closed in 1886.

Desire - The post office opened in 1877 and closed in 1878.

Germantown - Four miles east and two miles north of Yoder, it was said to have one of the best schools in Reno County. Locals also attended church. There was a carpenter, blacksmith and a hide dealer, as well as a ball club.

Huntsville - It had a post office from 1878 to 1905. It also had a store, a Methodist church, dance hall, pool hall, blacksmith, hotel, doctor and two country stores. There also was a school.

Jordan Springs - Located about two miles west and one mile south of Langdon, or 30 miles southwest of Hutchinson, Jordan Springs had a school, a store and a beauty shop. The post office opened in 1875 and closed in 1887.

Kent – In 1882, at least 25 people were living in Kent, located seven miles east of Hutchinson. It had a school and the rail-

The cemetery is all that remains of Sego, located in southern Reno County.

road went close by it. The post office opened in 1882, closed in 1901 and reopened in 1902, only to close again in 1904.

Leonville – The short-lived town had a post office in 1873, but it closed less than six months later. The town was six miles west of Partridge.

Leslie – Located 1.5 miles east of present-day Medora, the town had a post office that opened in 1874 and closed for three months in 1880. After it reopened, it closed in 1887.

Loda Center – This town was between Lerado and Pretty Prairie, at the intersection of Pretty Prairie Road and Hodge Road. It had a school with an enrollment of 34 in the early 1900s.

Marietta – The post office opened in 1878 and closed in 1887.

Mona – This town, a German Mennonite settlement, was on the Ninnescah River about five miles west of Ost, or St. Joe. The post office opened in 1879 and closed in 1901.

Mount Liberty – It was located on the south side of the Arkansas River, four miles northeast of Yoder. The post office opened in 1873. There also were two general stores and a school. There also were two other schools, Laurel and Olive, in the area. The post office closed in 1886.

Myton – This town was 25 miles northwest of Hutchinson on Peace Creek. There also was a school in the area.

New Boston – In 1879, a family looking for a suitable place to live bought land at the site of this town. Soon, there were eight homes on the south side of the section. But the families who lived there became discouraged and moved away. The town was 18 miles west of Hutchinson.

New Haven – The town's name was actually spelled New Heaven on its application for a post office. The town, three miles west and five miles north of Ost, or St. Joe, got its post office in 1877. It closed in 1887.

New London – The town was part of Rice County until the county line changed and it became part of Reno County. The post office opened in 1873 and closed in 1881.

Noblesville – It was founded in April 1930 by N.M. Begeman, who ran a filling station and grocery store. The Noblesville station, often still called the Huntsville Station, was converted

Amy Bickel/The Hutchinson News

into a private dwelling.

Og – Ten miles west of Castleton, it was named for a biblical giant who lived during the time of Moses. The post office opened in 1880 and closed in 1882.

Olcott – Six miles southwest of Lerado, the town was once called Dresden when it was in Kingman County, but when the Reno County boundary moved south, Dresden became part of Reno County and its name changed to Olcott. The post office opened in 1887 and closed in 1903. It reopened again in 1904 and closed in 1907.

The population in 1910 was 53. It was an important stop for the Missouri Pacific Railroad, because it was a coal and water station for the old steam locomotives. It had a depot, telegraph and express office, hotel, grocery store, Methodist church, grain elevator and a school. It even had a newspaper at one time, called the Weekly Press.

Ost – The town, typically known as St. Joe today, still has St. Joseph's Catholic Church. Back in the 1870s and 1880s, the town had a blacksmith, a barber and nearly 150 people.

Purity – It was located 22 miles south of Hutchinson, or about eight miles from Castleton. Locals talked a local couple into starting a country store and a post office. Neighbors hauled lumber to build the store free of charge. The name chosen for the post office was Therry Grove, but it was rejected. A local woman then chose the name Purity. The store opened in 1879 and the post office opened in 1880. There also was a blacksmith shop and a gristmill. An 1883 edition of The Hutchinson News stated, "Purity is booming." However, the post office closed in 1893.

Red Rock – This town was two miles southwest of present-day Plevna. It didn't have a post office, but it had an active Grange.

Riverside – Riverside was platted on the bank of the north fork of the Ninnescah River, one mile east of the old town of Arlington, by a young Julian E. Eaton in the early 1880s. He was sure the Rock Island would go through his town. He had streets named Parade, Ninnescah, Look Out Avenue and Highland Avenue. The town died, and Eaton went to Arlington, where he became the first mayor of the town at age 23.

Riverton – The post office opened in 1875 and closed in 1890.

Stella – The post office opened March 24, 1884 and closed in May 1886. It was located in the northwest corner of Haven Township. It was platted in 1885. When a railroad didn't go through the town and instead went through Haven, Stella folded.

Whiteside – Whiteside began in 1875 as a stop on the Sun City Trail. It once was called Sherman. A 1902 map listed it as Sherman Siding. The town once had a blockhouse, general store, stockyard, blacksmith, butcher and smokehouse. Whiteside still has an elevator. The coop was formed in 1915 and the present elevator built in 1953. And the blacksmith shop is still there, according to Newton.

Yaggy (Salem, Bath, Fruit Valley) – Situated on the Atchison, Topeka and Santa Fe Railroad, it was known as Salem when it was settled in 1872 and as Bath, Fruit Valley and eventually, Yaggy. It is believed that the Santa Fe Railroad changed the name to Bath following a bad train wreck in the area on Oct. 2, 1882. The mail train ran onto a sidetrack at Salem, waiting for the Cannon Ball to pass, but the switch was incorrectly turned and, with the Cannon Ball "tearing along at the rate of forty miles an hour," crashed into the mail train.

The town later became Fruit Valley and, by 1900, it was called Yaggy.

According to an Oct. 30, 1988, story in The News, Levi Walter Yaggy, a Chicago publisher, came to the area in 1884 to hunt geese. On his way back, he and his hunting friends saw a man digging for water about five miles northwest of Hutchinson. He asked how far down it would take to hit water and the man said 8 feet. Yaggy's hunting partners went back to Chicago and Yaggy purchased 1,500 acres of land and planted 400 acres of catalpa tress and 80,000 apple trees before returning to Chicago. Son Edward Yaggy came to the area in 1897 for a three-month stay, while his father was in Europe. He stayed 40 years.

In 1915, Yaggy sold 210,000 bushels of apples and added cowpeas, potatoes and sweet potatoes to the offerings. Yaggy Station soon became the largest shipping point for fruit between the Missouri River and California. A drought in 1930 killed the apple trees. They weren't replanted, with the farm instead growing more traditional crops.

Yaggy is near Willowbrook.

Signs still mark the location of Elmer, a Reno County ghost town. It consists of just a couple of houses and an old elevator.

Amy Bickel/The Hutchinson News

Calista

❖ Kingman County ❖

Mansion still stands, one of the few remains at Calista

Sunlight flickered through a window of the old mansion, showing off the faded pink flowered wallpaper in what once might have been a parlor.

Formerly the home of a rich cattle baron, hints of affluence linger in other rooms. The ornate woodwork trim still outlines doorways and a stained-glass window accents a room near the dining area. A few light fixtures hang from some rooms and an intricate brick fireplace that once sported a bearskin rug near the hearth – a prize of the owner's out-of-state hunt – looks as if it could still provide heat.

"If this house could talk … my, the story it could tell," said farmer Julius Govert, who traipsed through the inside of the 14-room mansion that sits on his property on a fall day.

Yet those who lived here are long gone and the empty home, marked by a long and winding tree-lined drive of several-decades-old cottonwood trees, is one of the few traces that Calista, Kansas, exists.

Take a trip down Highway 54 to a rural part of Kingman County, not far from the state fishing lake or the Byron Walker Wildlife Refuge. A green highway sign marks the incorporated town where three or four homes still stand, as well as an old blacksmith shop. A dilapidated sign points to the spot where an outdated elevator once stood – the local co-op finally tearing down the structure around the year 2009, after members built new concrete silos six miles away.

Although little is here, the town's mystique remains, whether it's the talk of how the cattle baron stole another man's wife or about grueling murders that happened in the mid- 20th century.

Old Calista, new Calista

In 1886, Henry Bennett deeded the land for the first Calista. Local historians say it was named after his wife, although, according to a historical document written by Govert's wife, Isabel, the wife's name was Mary Frances.

The first town had a post office, a two-story hotel, blacksmith shop, mill and a millrace – boasting a population of about 100 people before Bennett left town and cattle rancher John Arrington had another idea in mind.

As the story goes, the cowboy stole the wife of J.S. Betz. Betz's wife, Frances, said she'd marry Arrington if he built her a home of grandeur. He did and Frances moved half of the Betz barn to the Arrington Ranch, where it still stands today – part

of her divorce settlement, said Govert.

"She didn't want to live in some old shack," Govert said with a laugh, calling Mrs. Arrington "quite a regal lady."

With a new bride at home, Arrington decided to move the town of Calista, which had been a prospering community for roughly 15 years. Selling and shipping cattle, he wanted a depot and stockyards closer to his ranch, which was located a mile to the east. There were naysayers, but Arrington was successful in fording the town's buildings across the river to the newly platted site.

At least, it's the story that locals like Govert tell. Govert's wife, who handwrote the history on junk mail and scratch paper before her passing in 2009, noted Arrington had 700 to 1,000 head of cattle and at least three sections of crops – making him one of the wealthiest producers in the area.

The couple never had children for the big house, said 92-year old Beulah Graber, who grew up in the town before getting married and moving just a dozen miles away to the town of Zenda.

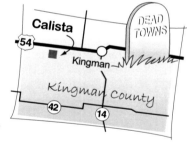

Location: Nine miles west of Kingman and about 1/2 mile south of U.S. 54/400 on SW 90th Avenue.

The Great Depression eventually hit Arrington, starting with the late 1920s collapse of the cattlemarket. He eventually lost the ranch and home not long before he died in 1933, Govert said.

A close-knit community

Despite Arrington's misfortunes, Calista continued into the 1930s, and Graber recalled the Old Settlers picnics that once happened on the lawn of the former Arrington home. Other entertainment included boxing and wrestling matches in the mercantile's upper story.

There also were annual rodeos, she said.

"I remember we'd climb up on the fence and take a look at those longhorns," Graber said. "There was a lot going on in Calista, actually, for such a small town."

The town had a small but stable economy of seven or eight

Calista

Photos by Amy Bickel/The Hutchinson News

The Arrington mansion was built by former cattle baron John Arrington with 14 rooms, stained glass window accents and ornate woodwork trim. The home was reroofed five years ago.

little businesses, many of which provided for the region's farmers, she said. Arrington started the lumberyard. There also was a coal yard, hardware store and post office.

Calista never was a bustling town, however. There were just a half-dozen families who called it home during her time there. Her father managed the town's two elevators, she said, noting he and her brother were murdered in the family's home after she had married and moved to Zenda.

Graber, however, didn't dwell on the topic, waving her hand in the air and saying it was another story for another time.

According to a May 1947 Hutchinson News story, two former carnival workers were charged with killing W.W. McClellan, 60, and his 36-year-old son, Arnold. The elder McClellan had picked up the transients a few days before the murders, hiring them to tar the elevator roof. The pair netted only $4.50 from the killings, according to the newspaper accounts. They were hanged July 29, 1947.

Julius Govert stands inside the Arrington mansion, a 14-room home built by John Arrington for his wife, Frances.

Life continues, somewhat

Now a meteorologist at KSN Channel 3, Mark Bogner grew up in the 1970s and 1980s less than two miles from Calista on his grandparents' farm. It's where his mother, Maureen, still lives.

He said he remembers a man running a blacksmith shop back then, and he and his family would take grain to the elevator. But with the county seat, Kingman, just 10 miles away, there was no need for a town like Calista.

"At the turn of the 20th century, there was a town every 10 miles," Bogner said, noting farmers and residents didn't want to travel more than 10 miles by horse or wagon to do business. "But as cars came along, every other little town went away – towns like Calista, Cairo – those little in-between towns diminished."

With the closing of the elevator, farmers are hauling their crops to the newest Calista – the Calista branch of the Cairo Co-op Equity Exchange a half-dozen miles away, said Julius' son, Dave Govert, who farms in the area.

Most have forgotten there ever was an old Calista – the first Calista – he said, noting the millrace still is visible at the abandoned site. The new elevator makes him wonder if future generations will someday forget about the present Calista. After all, Calista's current features might eventually disappear altogether, leaving it in the condition of many of the nearly 6,000 ghost towns in Kansas – dead.

Julius Govert has hope that Calista's story will live on. His wife wanted the same thing. She also loved the old Arrington home, which she and her first husband, Lee Osner, purchased in the 1970s.

Wanting to renovate the old mansion, she asked a builder to inspect it.

"He told them for what it would cost to fix up, he could build them a nice, new home much cheaper," Govert said, noting that is exactly what the couple did.

They built a new house beside the old one. Isabel had a new roof put on the Arrington estate about five years ago.

"She didn't want to see it fall in," he said.

Cleveland

❖ Kingman County ❖

Founders dreamed of the next Cleveland, Ohio. Instead Kansas
town that vied for Kingman County seat is no longer

Paul Handkins laughs when he recalls picking up his future wife for a date on a Sunday evening, only to be put off until she had played the piano at Cleveland Methodist Church.

Eventually, he would marry Dorothy on Dec. 31, 1944, in that same little church in Kingman County – about 20 years before it would be razed.

The vanished church, however, is just one of many structures to disappear in Cleveland. On a warm winter day, the couple drove around the former bustling town. There might be a foundation or two left of the church, but it was hard to tell through the sea of grass. Rubble and concrete from the old school, torn down a few years ago, are piled nearby, while any traces of a drugstore, lumberyard, livery and mercantile are nonexistent.

Paul Handkins points out the only remains of the town on the tour – a brick bank now used to store farm machinery and the elevator, built in the 1950s.

"It probably is one of the busiest elevators in the area," said local Paul Mitchell, who managed the location for 33 years. "There's nothing but wheat fields for miles and miles and miles."

But when the June harvest ends, the town's activity goes back into dormancy.

Dreams of a county seat

When founders platted the town, they had dreams of a city that would prosper like Cleveland, Ohio.

Thus, they named it Cleveland in 1879 – a town in the geographic center of Kingman County. Founders hoped to secure the county seat and a great railroad center.

However, while locals called it Cleveland, the Santa Fe Railroad called it Carvel or Carvil because shipping was becoming confusing between the Kansas town and one in Oklahoma.

The railroad's name didn't seem to stick with residents, however. A newspaper, the Cleveland Star, was established by P.J. Conklin to help the county seat cause along, according to the Kingman County Historical Society. Then, a petition was sent to the county commissioners to relocate the county seat.

Kingman, six miles to the north, wasn't going to let the county seat go too quickly, Paul Handkins said. They worked out a deal with the nearby town of Dale to help swing the vote. The county had an election and Kingman secured a majority.

The newspaper eventually moved to Kingman; its name changed to the Republican.

It would be one of several disasters, it seems.

A cyclone struck Cleveland in 1885, destroying half a dozen houses and injuring several people. In 1887, a prairie fire swept over a portion of the township. Residents, however, didn't give up.

It had a drugstore, merchants, a real estate office, hotel, post office, livery and feed store, as well as a loan agent, mason, blacksmith and butcher, according to research at the Kingman Library. Cleveland had 80 people in 1887. While life wasn't simple for the pioneers, the town's growth continued into the 20th century.

The Kingman newspaper, in 1905, reported the dedication of a new church at Cleveland. In 1908, the paper reported that a large hotel would soon be erected on the corner of Broadway and Main streets. There also was a school and a second elevator.

Yet, while the town had a railroad and was centrally located, it began to dwindle. Seventy-five years after it was founded, the town had only a post office, an elevator, a school, a church and eight dwellings. The post office closed in 1957. The school closed a year later. Then, in 1967, the church closed as well.

Location: Cleveland is about six miles south of Kingman, approximately 3 miles west of Kansas Highway 14 on SW 10th Avenue.

Little left

A few homes remain in Cleveland, scattered about several blocks. One resident sells fresh eggs.

Paul Mitchell, who retired just a few years ago as the elevator manager, said there used to be a sign outside the elevator on the tracks marking the town as Carvel. One day, it just disappeared.

Cleveland's demise isn't unique, however, he said. Many other Kingman County towns have had the same fate.

Cleveland

Nothing is left of Alameda, just four miles to the east. Gage, renamed Basil by the railroad, is just a few miles to the southeast, and a dilapidated elevator along the railroad tracks is the last remnant of the town. Little remains of St. Leo, Belmont and Penalosa, among others.

Paul and Dorothy Handkins lived on a farm about 12 miles south of the town, but last year the couple decided to move closer to family in Wichita. Paul, who turned 90 in 2011, worked for several weeks during the winter to get ready for

his farm sale in late February 2011. He planned to sell the light fixture from the Methodist church – one of the last remnants of the place where he and his wife were married.

He misses the farm, he admitted as he peered out the car window. He also misses Cleveland.

"It's interesting to think about what it would be like if Dale hadn't helped Kingman and Cleveland would have won the county seat," he said.

From the Kingman Leader-Courier, August 5, 1909

Now that the scramble for nominations is over, all things are quiet about Cleveland, except the rush in business.

W. W. Magruder keeps a good assortment of dry goods, groceries, queensware glassware, flour, meal and drugs, which he is dispensing to his customers at a lively rate.

Frank Byers retains the respect of the farmers by keeping their plows sharp and their horses feet shod.

The Cleveland post office is still in the hands of E. Ozbun, notwithstanding his resignation and the effort that has been

put forth by the democrats to have a change in the office.

Rev. Thomas, of Kingman, preached a sermon to an appreciative audience last Sabbath in our town. There is preaching here nearly every Sunday afternoon, at the schoolhouse. We are talking up the subject of building a church house at this place.

If those young bloods who were running horse races in our streets last Sunday will refrain from disturbing the peace hereafter there will probably be nothing more said about it, but a word to the wise is sufficient.

Wheat harvest makes the town bustle in June. The elevator is the last business in town.

Photos by Amy Bickel/The Hutchinson News

Above: Cleveland was founded in 1879 with the hopes of gaining the county seat. It lost the election to Kingman and now the unincorporated town has just a few dwellings, along with an elevator.

An old outhouse still stands in the backyard of a residence in Cleveland.

Waterloo

❖ Kingman County ❖

Waterloo's claim to fame: It has the oldest arboretum west of the Mississippi.

The government said the trees John Walter Riggs requested would never grow in Kansas.

Grandson and namesake John Riggs chuckled at this statement as he stood amid 10 acres of timber, gesturing to four sturdy Bald Cypress trees that are well beyond 100 years in age – a few of the saplings the U.S. Department of Agriculture said could not grow in a climates like Kansas.

Not that the naysayer theories weren't warranted. After all, when the elder Riggs, an Indiana native, first came to the small Kingman County town of Waterloo in the 1880s, there was nothing around it but barren prairie. The new Kansas pioneer, however, had visions for this vast sea of grass.

On a spring day in 2011, grandson Riggs, of Lindsborg, and his wife, Janie, walked the trails crisscrossing 10 acres of what is known as Riggs Arboretum– proclaimed to be the oldest arboretum west of the Mississippi. Thanks to his grandson and others, John Walter Riggs' legacy lives on in this little town.

Barren prairie to a grove of trees

As some jokingly said in the late 1800s, there was nothing between the homestead and the North Pole but a barbed-wire fence.

That is what John and Sarah Riggs found when they came to Waterloo in 1887, a tiny settlement about nine miles east of Kingman. The two were schoolteachers with aspirations of having a permanent home. They chose Waterloo because of the availability of teaching positions. They were among the residents with dreams of seeing their town thrive.

The first post office at this location was called Stanford. It was established March 5, 1878 – a Pony Express station located in the dugout of Simon F. Utley.

In 1881, the government changed the name of the post office to Waterloo. Within a few years, the town was booming.

The Feb. 27, 1885, issue of the Kingman Courier lists Waterloo as a thriving little town with a hotel, three general merchandise stores, a post office, blacksmith shop, wagon shop, livery stable and a broom factory supplied by 20 acres of broomcorn raised by Hugh McBride.

Eventually, there were churches, a jewelry and shoe store and a creamery, according to information documented by Irene Bergkamp.

Riggs and his wife settled into their new home in their new town, but Riggs still dreamed of his trees of the east. He began ordering fruit trees and fruit-bearing shrubs from his home state of Indiana, according to "The History of the Waterloo Tree Farm."

He began the Waterloo nursery in 1887 – not long after settling in the area - and soon was growing plants from all over the United States to see how they fared in Kansas. In 1899, he asked USDA officials for a variety of trees from overseas to try in his arboretum. Scientists there repeatedly told him the varieties he sought could not grow in Kansas.

Yet Riggs persisted until the USDA finally agreed to send the trees and, along with them, an investigator, John's grandson said.

They must have been impressed, he added, because the department began issuing his grandfather trees and decided to make the arboretum a federal experiment station.

The USDA appointed his grandfather as superintendent. News began to spread beyond the tiny town.

"John W. Riggs, government forester, has a wonderful collection of trees and plants," reported the Kingman Journal in 1901. "Among them are cedars of Lebanon, Olive of Palestine, sequoia, magnolia, plants from Australia and the lotus from the Nile. ... He has succeeded in making a number of rare plants grow, some of which had never before been cultivated in this country."

Riggs supervised the arboretum even after federal funding for the station ran out in the 1920s. He died in 1930 in a fire that took his home, which was at the arboretum.

Son Cecil, who operated a commercial nursery business in Kingman, took over the work of preserving the arboretum. Cecil died in 1962.

Cecil had developed the same passion for nature, the

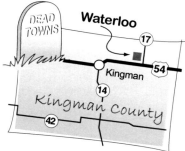

Location: On the intersection of NE 20th and NE Waterloo Avenue – about a mile west of Highway 17 in Kingman County.

Waterloo

John Riggs, and his wife Janie, walk through the arboretum his grandfather, also named John Riggs, started in 1887 at the now ghost town of Waterloo. Riggs Arboretum is presumed to be the oldest arboretum west of the Mississippi.

younger John Riggs said of his father. He remembers sitting in is his father's 1940s pickup, watching locals cut away some of his grandfather's trees that had been in the Waterloo town square park. It wasn't long after the end of World War II, and veterans who came home wanted a place to play baseball.

Tears welled in Cecil's eyes. There were a few cuss words, Riggs said. His father looked at the trees with the same love as his grandfather – trees that had been growing for more than 50 years.

Nevertheless, Riggs added, "They needed a place to play and, I have to admit, they got a lot of use out of the ball diamond for many, many years."

A monument to Kansas' natural history

The ballpark, these days, is not played on very often – though bases, a pitching mound and home plate still rest in the well-kept infield. St. Louis Catholic Church still has Saturday evening services and parishioners use the old parochial school as a community building. Local women still meet every Wednesday to quilt in the school's upstairs.

In 1888, the town had 200 people. Today, however, only a few houses circle the old town square, including one that once served as the public school.

As for the remaining business community, there is a local man who restores cars in a shop.

John Riggs said he grew up in Kingman before heading to school to become a city planner and landscape architect – a passion he figures he developed in the grove of trees at Waterloo. As a child growing up in the 1950s, John Riggs helped his father maintain the arboretum. And, like many children, Riggs would have rather been doing something else at the time.

"I asked my father why we were doing this and he said, 'Sometimes you do things because it is the right thing to do.' "

Riggs has never forgotten those words. His father died in the 1960s, but Riggs continued to care for the acreage.

It took years to get it back into shape, he said. After his father died, the arboretum was abandoned for a time and the processes of nature took its toll. It was overgrown with brush and weeds, so John and Janie Riggs and their children began to work to preserve it.

The family now has two workdays a year – one in the fall and one in the spring – with volunteers coming from across the region to help maintain the historical grove.

Riggs himself has become an arborist of sorts, the love of the tree passed down to a third generation. At the entrance of the arboretum, he points out a Japanese Eucommia – one of the oldest in the state.

"It's exactly what my grandfather would have wanted," John Riggs said. "He died a poor man, but he left behind a legacy."

Runnymede

❖ Harper County ❖

***Settlement was a continuous Mardi Gras for
English gentry during its short lifespan***

Life was so good in Runnymede that the young British gentry forgot to go to work.

Their fathers had sent them to learn about farming on the plains of Kansas – paying $500 a year as well as sending remittances to their sons.

Yet, instead, life in this little town seemed to be a modern-day Mardi Gras. The rich Englishmen partied and played sports like tennis and rugby. They had cockfights and a racetrack. There also was a hotel, a soda-water bottle plant and bowling alley.

These days on the Kansas prairie, there are no traces of the drinking and playtime for a few hundred young men. The land now is fields farmed by local farmer Mike Newsum. Occasionally, Newsum finds pieces of pop bottles from the old soda plant on the site. In the past, some have found English coins.

The tale of Runnymede is one that has been passed down through the years and even was written into a book by a settler's relative – "They Had a Good Time While It Lasted," said Gail Bellar, a member of the Harper County Historical Society who has researched the town.

"I think it is a fascinating story," she said.

Turnly's scheme

Maybe he was a man who sat up at night dreaming of how to make a quick buck.

Or, maybe he truly thought he'd do some good on his newly purchased ranch on the Chikaskia River near the Kingman-Harper county line.

Nonetheless, Irishman Francis "Ned" Turnly had a plan – or a scheme – some might say. Around 1887, he established the town of Runnymede, about 13 miles northeast of Harper and just west of the river in Harper County where he began his venture.

He knew a lot about wayward sons of British sires. Their sons were hard riders and hard drinkers and when it came to matters of business, they really didn't show much interest, according to the book "When Kansas Was Young," by Thomas Allen McNeal. Turnly went to their fathers with his proposition.

"Out of the great wide and fertile plains of the central part of the United States, there is the opportunity to develop these sons of yours and build up a rich English colony which will be an honor to the British Empire and a credit to your family," Turnly said.

And, just like many who tried to grow towns on the state's landscape, he painted a picture of sunsets, land with rich soil and a place where these young men could learn the trade of farming and ranching. All they needed, he said, was a course under an able instructor, according to McNeal's book.

Runnymede appealed to the parents, largely because it required a fee high enough to guarantee that no riffraff would be admitted, Bellar said. It was in a location in Kansas with prohibition laws and it was named Runnymede, in honor of England. Turnly's plan worked and this little oasis in Harper County began to grow. It is said the town covered as many as seven city blocks with houses mostly of the English style. The residences even had hedges.

A British remittance man named Robert Watmough helped push the town's expansion. He started several businesses then sold them, Bellar said. That included the soda water bottling plant, which, according to one report, made 19 different flavors.

There was a stage that made daily trips to Norwich and Harper. The framed hotel had rates higher than Kansas City. There was a church, stores, bowling alley and livery. Cigars sold for 25 cents each, according to Kansas State Historical Society documents.

The English, however, weren't learning much about agriculture, according to the documents. They built a racetrack and ground for hurdle races, which attracted large crowds, according to the documents. They partied and drank, just like they did in England. Liquor was shipped in by wagon.

On one occasion, they hoisted the English flag above the American flag and a riot started. The flag was taken down with apologies made by Turnly and others.

"The news spread over the state and for several months people came from western Kansas and other parts of the state in

Location: Northeast corner of Harper County near the Kingman/Harper county line.

Runnymede

covered wagons and occasionally on horseback, offering their services to drive out the English," according to the documents.

Despite some public outcry, Turnly's plans for the town continued, and he and others dreamed the railroad would run south from Hutchinson.

However, according to the documents, populism and other kinds of political views kept the railroad out of Runnymede. The state's citizens saw an imaginary danger in allowing too much foreign money into Kansas. Turnly's plans soon began to go downhill.

On May 1, 1890, a fire burned the livery. Robert Watmough, the influential promoter and citizen who had been partying that night and was sleeping off his inebriation in a stable, died in the fire. Watmough is buried in a cemetery at Harper.

"The story is that he was engaged to one of Ned Turnly's sisters," Bellar said, noting that Watmough was planning to leave for his wedding in England in a few days. "They had this big party at the hotel. He went to the stables to sleep and then a fire broke out."

By this time, the young Brits' fathers were getting tired of the stipends, and they probably had heard reports of what actually was going on in the town of Runnymede. They brought their sons home. By mid-1892, Turnly's real estate holdings were declared vacated for nonpayment of taxes, according to Runnymede Hotel's website. By 1893, the colonists had gone.

The church was moved to Harper and still stands as a museum. The hotel was moved to Alva, Okla., the third story torn off. It still stands, serving as a community meeting place.

"I think he knew the end was coming anyway," Bellar said

of Turnly. "These younger sons, they weren't successful farmers. They would get checks from England to keep them going. They didn't have a lot of incentive to try."

As English Runnymede vanished, a new Runnymede, south of English Runnymede, eventually sprang up along a railroad. There was a school, elevator and store there, Bellar said. Only in name was this Runnymede affiliated with Turnly's English town.

Just a memory

There are no traces of foundations, tennis courts or much else on the former Runnymede site, said Harper County farmer Newsum. Buildings were sold to pay debts and Turnly left Kansas. What remains today is the church and the hotel, which is located 50 miles south.

Newsum said he sometimes sees pieces of glass glimmering in the sunlight when he's out on the tractor. It could be from the soda-water bottling plant or it could be the liquor bottles. Other than that, only an unmarked grave of Thomas Hudson remains, along with a Kansas State Historical Society marker.

Relatives of Hudson told Newsum, who farms their ground, that Hudson and his family stayed the winter in Runnymede on their way to warmer climates. He eventually died and, for several decades, a fence outlined the small burial plot.

About 40 or 50 years ago, his family moved the stone, placing it next to his wife's grave, Newsum said. He said Runnymede these days is nothing more than a wheat field.

"People say, and I haven't seen it with my own eyes, but if you were in an airplane at the right time of year with the wheat, you can still see the indentions of the track," Bellar said.

The church in Runnymede was moved to Harper and still stands as a museum.

Courtesy Kanss State Historical Society

Freeport

❖ Harper County ❖

State's smallest incorporated city still kicking with just five official residents

It mirrors what some consider a ghost town with just four houses, a street lined with empty storefronts and a former school building that is falling into disrepair. Moreover, the state's tiniest hamlet, sandwiched between wheat fields and pasture grasses in Harper County, has only five official residents.

Yet Carol Peterson would argue with anyone that Freeport, Kansas, couldn't be a ghost town - not with a mayor and four council members - a core group of residents with a passion to keep the town on the map.

"When I think of dead towns, I think of towns that are not even there anymore," she said as she and a half dozen area residents gathered in the Freeport City Hall for their weekly coffee and chatter. "The surrounding people who live here, this is home to them."

Peterson, who grew up near Freeport and attended the elementary school, won't disagree that life here is well passed its heyday, however. At one time in the late 1800s, Freeport had more than 700 inhabitants. There was a bank, two hotels, two newspapers, five dry good stores, nine grocery stores, three drugstores, two hardware stores and two elevators, among other businesses. The town even boasted a police force for a time.

Nevertheless, one by one, those businesses closed. The once bustling Main Street sees high traffic only during the harvest season as trucks head toward the last remaining business - the co-op. The school closed decades ago and the bank, which once gave Freeport its title as "the smallest incorporated city in the United States with a bank" left town 1 1/2 years ago, setting up a location in the nearby county seat town of Anthony, 13 miles to the west.

Meanwhile, when the previous mayor and her husband left the state five years ago, Peterson and her husband, Bill, who moved back to the area in the mid-1980s, had their property annexed into the city to keep the five-member city government going.

Now, residents are grappling with losing another one of the last remnants of their little town's existence, which has been in place since Freeport's incorporation in 1885.

In April 2011, government officials met with locals to discuss the possibility of closing the post office.

Those gathering for their weekly Thursday coffee at the bank-turned-City Hall discussed the fact. Inside, a sign pinned to the wall reads "Help Keep Our Post Office - Buy Stamps."

"Last year, the bank moved into a bigger city to keep themselves in business and this year it looks like the post office is going to go," Bill Peterson, who has served as mayor the past five years, said. "And I don't know what we can do to stop it from happening."

Hard luck

Freeport is the smallest of Kansas' 627 incorporated cities.

In the town's post office, with 1920s-era decor and 80 post office boxes, locals have just eight boxes rented, Terry Ball, the post office's officer in charge, said in May 2011. He said there was a time when almost every box was occupied.

Freeport's post office has history, after all - a story that involves a bitter battle with the town across the street, Mid Lothian. It was back when Freeport wasn't quite as small - when dreams here included commerce, houses filled with families and children in the school.

Back then, towns were situated every 10 miles - a good distance for farmers to travel by horse to do their business.

Location: About six miles south of U.S. 160 on NE 100 Avenue in eastern Harper County

Freeport's beginnings were somewhat shaky. The railroad didn't go through where Mid Lothian founders had situated their town. Thus, B.H. Freeman moved his post office, which had been in existence since 1879, two miles to the southeast, right next to the eight-day-old town of Freeport. Freeman was the one who named it Mid Lothian, a Scottish word that means mid-ocean or mid-land, according to Freeport historical articles.

The locations of both cities were too close together for residents to stay civil. Freeport and Mid Lothian sat side by side. Freeport's Main Street was two blocks north of Mid Lothian's Main Street, with the two towns joined by Grand Avenue.

Freeport

Officer in Charge Terry Ball at the Freeport post office takes care of his duties in the mornings at the office in the state's smallest incorporated city.

Hostility grew, especially over who would get the railroad depot. When it went on Freeport's side, tension peaked and, as local lore says, residents went as far as to build a fence down the middle of Grand Avenue and dared either side to cross it.

Eventually leaders from the communities met and came to an agreement. Mid Lothian would give up its name, as well as give Freeport its post office, in exchange for the opening of a vacant strip of land between the two towns that provided a needed street for Mid Lothians that gave them access to the depot.

Freeport immediately doubled in size and, by the spring of 1892, there were 700 people in the city. However, by September 1893, Freeport's population plummeted as residents took advantage of the Cherokee Strip Run for free land in Oklahoma, which is 13 miles to the south.

A census report from 1894 showed only 54 people living in Freeport. In 1910, population peaked again at 161 residents, then began to fall.

Freeport's population even dropped since the 2000 census, when the town had six people.

City Clerk Jim Brooks, the last resident in town who has lived in Freeport his entire 73 years of life, has watched the community dwindle. His mother ran a grocery and his father worked at the bank.

He recalls attending the Freeport elementary school and playing jacks with his friends in front of the grocery. Sometimes, when it was cold, he and his friends would roller skate in the store. Occasionally, he would lead his horse into the store, feeding it candy.

"My mother was on my tail with a broom," he laughed. "It didn't take long to get the horse out."

The horse would even leave his mother "a few gifts," he said.

"She had a broom and a shovel, I think," he said with a chuckle.

The issue of closing Freeport's post office surfaced in the past but the public outcry was so loud government officials backed off. But Brooks, who on a recent morning pointed out the town's landmarks as he stood near the location of his parents' store, doesn't know that the city will put up a similar fight.

Freeport's post office has helped keep the town's rural identity. Those who gather every Thursday make sure to buy stamps in an effort to boost the office's revenue.

Brooks, however, said he knows it is probably not enough to keep it going.

"I hate to see it go, but that's progress, I think," he said.

Still hanging on

Few, except for locals, remember Mid Lothian. It's now a ghost town, remembered mostly in the annuals of Freeport history.

Other Harper County towns that lost post offices also have disappeared - towns with names like Crystal Springs, Camchester, Joppa and Swan.

Yet, unlike the dozens of towns that have been swept off the map in Harper County, Freeport's residents have a will to survive - all five of them and then some - whether there is a post office or no post office, Carol Peterson said.

For those who can attend, there is the weekly socializing at City Hall. Meanwhile, the church still opens its doors every Sunday, drawing in more than 30 people from the town and surrounding farmsteads every week. It has a membership of more than 50.

"I believe the church has kept this community together more than anything else," Carol Peterson said, adding that

Freeport

there also is a certain nostalgia about Freeport that brings former residents back into town for a visit.

"Many people have moved away, but we have visitors every weekend who come back to go by the old school, go into the church, look at the church again," she said. "People enjoy coming back to the small city, to an easier, simpler time in life. It is just home to them. They come back to their roots."

Dick Busby, Anthony, who has been the pastor at Freeport's Presbyterian Church for three years, said it's easy to see what makes the town special – remarking on Freeport's longstanding tradition and its sense of homecoming.

His wife, Diana, said it is the country feel that lingers here that she loves.

When Kansas Gov. Sam Brownback touted his rural opportunity zone plan in 2011 with a hope to draw out-of-state residents

Photo courtesy Carol Peterson

Freeport's Main Street in a photograph from 1906.

to rural Kansas – Bill Peterson said he's received a number of calls from people across the United States wanting to move to tiny Freeport – wanting to live in a place with a quiet, uncomplicated lifestyle. The only problem is there are no homes available.

Richard and Bonnie Strickland took advantage of the only vacant property in November. They knew someone who was looking for a couple to rent a home just south of Freeport and fix it up.

Richard Strickland, a military veteran who grew up in Oswego in southeast Kansas, jumped at the chance to move out of the state's largest city of Wichita.

"You move to a city and the city swallows you up," he said. "This is Americana. It's great to live in the United States of America, and this is where our country has come from – from farming the earth and living off the earth. This is like where I grew up in southeast Kansas – the closest thing since I left home."

Sandra J. Milburn/The Hutchinson News

Jim Brooks, left, the town's clerk, Pat Coady, Richard and Bonnie Strickland, Pastor Dick and Diana Busby, Mayor Bill Peterson and Carol Peterson all stand outside of Freeport's Presbyterian Church.

Fremont

❖ McPherson County ❖

*The oldest public structure in McPherson County,
the little stone church still embodies the history of Fremont.*

There was talk at one time of tearing it down – the little stone church that sometimes is overlooked because of the mammoth one beside it.

The prairie church, after all, hadn't really been used in years. For a while, members of the congregation filled it with storage.

"That would have been sad," Lindsborg resident Orvin Lundquist, 90, said of the possible razing, noting there is just too much history in the now 141-year-old building to reconsider the matter.

After all, he noted, tiny Freemount Lutheran Church was one of the first structures his Swedish ancestors built when they settled the empty prairie in 1869. He recalls the story of his great-grandfather, John Rodell, going from neighbor to neighbor telling them there would be a meeting about building a church.

In fact, it's the oldest public structure still in use in McPherson County. Once a year, on Labor Day Sunday, the congregation leaves the confines of the bigger, stately brick building for a historical service in the much smaller, prairie-built quarters of the little stone church.

The churches sit in the middle of the phantom town of Fremont - named after explorer John Fremont, who trekked through Kansas on government expeditions.

Their future town and church needed a name, and they decided at the time that Fremont was a worthy title, said Freemount's pastor, the Rev. Jim Harrison. However, church members eventually changed the name of their church to Freemount because they didn't like the explorer's political views.

Not much is left of the town of Fremont, which sits between Marquette and Lindsborg in McPherson County. The church

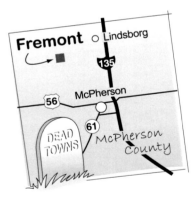

Location: Fremont is 1.5 miles south of Highway 4 on Eighth Avenue.

buildings, a cemetery and a few houses are the last remains of where its Swedish founders had dreams of a bustling city.

However, Harrison said, those surrounding the community are working to keep their heritage alive - a focus centered on the old stone church that nearly disappeared in the 1980s.

Swedish roots

Lundquist, currently Freemount's longest serving member, said his ancestors came from Sweden to Illinois before traveling to Kansas where land already had been set aside for the homesteaders. At that time, the grass was tall enough that one pioneer even got lost amid it while journeying back from Salina.

They lived in dugouts until they could build their own homes - even meeting for church services in a dugout until the first services could be held in May 1870.

The community built the church using sandstone from the surrounding Smoky Hills, hauling it on heavy sleds. Then they mixed mortar from nearby Paint Creek, which made the stone as hard as concrete, Lundquist said.

When it was first built, the immigrants could not afford to put on a roof, he said.

"They put some branches on top to shade the people," he said. "They didn't have a floor for a while, either, and each farm family made their own benches and put them in the church."

One story Lundquist shared was a Sunday service where the sanctuary began to get darker and darker. They looked out the windows and saw Indians staring back at them.

There never was any trouble, he said, noting that settlement of the Kansas landscape continued.

It didn't take long for the congregation to outgrow the church. In 1881, members built a larger structure, Lundquist said. He was 6 years old on June 7, 1926 when lightning struck the high steeple, burning the church. Families, however, salvaged much from the church, including the pews, while the church burned.

New church, old church

A third, gothic-style church made of red brick was completed in 1927. The newest church and the oldest church stand nearly side-by-side, a contrast between a building erected out of necessity and one built with enough time to plan for ornate

Fremont

details such as stained glass and a Birger Sandzen painting at the altar.

Now the old stone church is a museum, said Lois Howe, a former Freemount member and past chairwoman of the Freemount Historical Society. Her ancestors also came to the area in 1869.

Artifacts from the second sanctuary, including the gold cross from the spire, a baptismal bowl, candelabra and pews are in the building. Howe said they use the old pump organ when they meet in the church. Pictures on the walls chronicle the burning of the second church and other activities that have happened over the years.

And on Labor Day Sunday, Harrison said he dons a traditional black robe to make the service more historic.

Meanwhile, unlike the non-air-conditioned brick structure they use every Sunday, the old stone church has a climate-controlled system to keep the artifacts from decaying, Harrison said.

The church museum also contains old Fremont's history, including a plat map of the town and photos of the general store. A sign and postal boxes are from the old post office, which closed in 1932.

"Fremont did have a gas pump and a grocery store and a blacksmith shop," Lundquist said. "They had an elevator for wheat and panels for stock cattle. I drove a lot of cattle to Fremont and waited for the train."

He also frequented the store, sometimes buying candy, he said.

Lundquist said his great-grandfather Rodell is buried in the nearby cemetery - the only gravesite funded by congregation members because of the activities Rodell did to build and improve the church. He even preached on occasion when the church didn't have a minister.

Lundquist's daughter now lives on the 1869 homestead that his grandfather, who married Rodell's daughter, first proved up. It has now gone through four generations of farmers.

It is all part of his Swedish history that he and others here want to keep alive, he said. That makes keeping the little stone church going all the more important.

"It is a memory – a tribute to our founding fathers who started the church," he said. "We still think it is pretty precious."

File photos/The Hutchinson News

Above: The Freemount Lutheran Church was one of the first buildings Swedish immigrants built when they settled in Kansas in 1869. The old stone church is now used as a museum after a newer church was completed in 1927.

Right: Pastor Jim Harrison conducts services in the old stone church structure, the oldest building still in use in McPherson County.

Empire

❖ McPherson County ❖

New York jazz artist inspired by the town his relatives started – a town that ran the whole course of its history in under 10 years

He's never been to this unsheltered spot on the Kansas prairie where his ancestors settled – a town abandoned in the late 1870s when the railroad missed it.

But New York jazz bassist Scott Colley found inspiration for his new album from the McPherson County town that these days is nothing more than crop fields and grass.

It's a tale that had been passed down from one generation to the next – a tale his mother eventually handed down to him, he said while on tour in Sweden in fall 2010. The story centers on his great-great-grandfather Joseph Colby, who founded an "Empire" on the Kansas plains – the first settlement of McPherson County.

Old photograph

Colley already had been working on his latest album, one influenced by scenes of the Old West. But amid his work, he took down a copy of the photo hanging on his office wall his mother had given him. It showed Civil War veteran Joseph Colby and his family, including his great-grandmother Mary, outside their sod house at Empire.

Colley began to delve a bit into Empire's history – looking at information his uncle Harry Gadd, of Nevada, had researched. He learned of Empire's beginnings and of its ultimate demise.

According to Galva, Kansas, historical records:

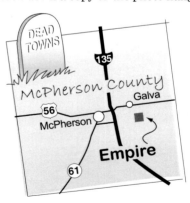

Location: One mile east and two miles south of Galva on 22nd Avenue.

In 1875 Joseph J. Colby constructed the first permanent residence, which was the beginning of Empire. Any hope for a prosperous future for Empire was shattered when a branch of the Atchison, Topeka and Santa Fe Railroad was completed September 23, 1879. It passed north of Empire,

through the present site of Galva. With the town missing the tracks, it didn't take long for the residents of Empire to move their buildings north to the new town site.

By 1880, even the post office was closed. The beginning of Galva meant the end of Empire.

– Galva, Kansas, Historical Records

The information was moving to Colley, who decided to change the name of his album to reflect his family history.

"The original title I had for the recording was 'Provenance," Colley said. "But once I found the quote online – "the end of Empire..." – I knew right away that that was the title. The idea kind of took over. This image it created for me – this family settling in this place in the middle of the Plains – it must have been an incredibly difficult life."

Leora Foster Flook described in a document about coming to Empire in 1873 at age 6. It's where her parents would stake a claim. They traveled by rail from Iowa to Newton - the end of the rail.

"Early the next morning we started for our new home in a lumber wagon behind a big span of mules," Flook wrote. "The road was only a track across the prairie marked by a row of little stakes with white rags on them. There were very few houses and nothing much to see but the rolling prairie, so the trip was rather tedious for we children."

It was a tough life, Flook wrote, noting that grasshoppers came in 1874.

"They darkened the windows like a cloud, ate holes in the flour and other things at the store. So had to cover everything possible. We had a small patch of sod corn but when the hoppers left, there was only a few little stalks left with no leaves on them. The chickens nearly run their legs off catching hoppers. Then they left as suddenly as they came."

That winter was very hard times for Kansas pioneers, Flook wrote. Many became discouraged and went back east and others had to have help.

According to Galva Historical Society documents, one pioneer wrote that for fuel, settlers gathered cow chips. Some burned cornstalks and corn. Some even prospected for coal.

"So far from established civilization. Starting from scratch and then naming this place Empire," Colley said. "They must

Empire

Amanda Loman/The Hutchinson News

The cemetery is one of the few remaining traces of the town of Empire.

have had some very big plans. And then, a few years later, the town just evaporates when the trains come through up north."

Empire, it seems, ran the whole course of its history in under 10 years.

Prairie Empire

These days, Empire is now just a spot covered by trees and farmland near the intersection of 22nd Avenue and Iron Horse Road in McPherson County, just southeast of Galva. All remnants are gone, except for a graveyard and a single marker constructed in memory of the town and area's prominence as a Santa Fe Trail stop.

Everything else was moved to nearby Galva when the town dissolved.

According to a paper written by a McPherson College student, Martin Nolan, in 1975, wagon trains passed the site of Empire as early as 1823, a junction for both the Santa Fe Trail and the California Road.

Linda Andersen, with the Galva Historical Museum, said the Empire site became more of a regular stop for travelers in 1855 when Charles Fuller built a ranch just west of Turkey Creek – the first settlement in McPherson County. It served as a place for them to water their stock, sleep and eat before heading west.

The government established a post office at the site from 1860 to 1866, according to the Kansas State Historical Society, and the area continued to be a stop along the trail system.

However, it was when Colley's great-great grandfather, Joseph Colby, his wife, Sarah, and their seven children came to the county and built a sod house at the ranch site in 1871

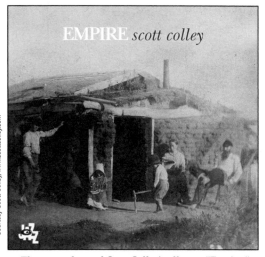

Courtesy Scott Colley, www.scottcolley.com

EMPIRE *scott colley*

The cover of one of Scott Colley's albums, "Empire," is a photo of the sod home belonging to his great-great-grandfather, Joseph Colby. The home was located at the site of Empire. The girl in the center, sitting, is Colley's great-grandmother, Mary.

that Empire began to prosper. Colby established a post office in his home in October 1872 and walked to Roxbury once a week to pick up and deliver the mail, according to Martin.

"He envisioned a big town," Andersen said of Colby's dreams – dreams that weren't uncommon on Kansas' sparsely populated landscape.

Martin also reported that The McPherson Messenger mentioned Empire as one of the county's growing communities.

"Empire City is situated eight miles east of McPherson, at the old Santa Fe crossing of Turkey Creek. The creek at this place is fed by springs which do not fail, making a very good location for a town on the account of the abundant supply of water."

And, for 10 years, the little community seemed to have a promising future. Structures included a school, mill, blacksmith shop and grocery, Andersen said, adding there were more than 20 buildings in all.

A couple of entrepreneurs attempted to mine coal, although, she said, their endeavor, except for finding traces, was unsuccessful. There was a church, as well as a doctor, druggist, real estate businessmen and a photographer. Meanwhile, extracurricular activities included a string band, literary club, a gun club and a baseball team, Martin wrote.

While Martin noted the town had a sheriff, there also were "minute men" who upheld the law. For instance, according to a newspaper account, a man who had been "taking improper liberties" with a neighbor's daughter received the wrath of Empire's minutemen. The mob shaved his head, horsewhipped him, and tar-and-feathered him. The man took the case to court for his treatment, eventually receiving about $100 of the $10,000 he requested.

"The implications of this case are many," Martin wrote. "It definitely tells us a lot about the psychology of the people of Empire. They were willing to take responsibility for the protection of their community and knew that law was necessary for a rewarding life. Their methods may be questionable, but they merely reflect the environment and way of life experienced by early settlers."

A town dies

Life, these first settlers would find, was tough on the desolate plains.

Plague after plague hit the area, including grasshoppers, a hailstorm and drought. Empire was narrowly missed by one wildfire, but hit by another. The first death came in 1873 when a man named Michael Sauer was caught in a blizzard searching for wood to warm his wife and baby. He never recovered, dying a month later. Sauer's grave became the first one in Empire Cemetery.

The ultimate demise, however, happened in September 1879 when the railroad missed town by just a few miles – what residents had been hoping for several months would be the town's saving grace, Andersen said.

Thus, one by one, residents moved to the tracks, to what was a railroad campsite. They named it Galva.

According to Martin's research, there were at least 20 buildings at Galva by 1880, while Empire was nearly deserted. In fact, the State Board of Agriculture's Fourth Biennial Report in 1883-84 didn't list Empire on the map.

Still a memory

Most have forgotten this little town, Andersen said, noting the land has been farmed and remains are few.

A Brethren church in McPherson has ties to Empire. Meanwhile, at least one home still stands in Galva that was moved from the Empire site when the town disappeared.

There's also a low spot in the road that marks where the coal mine probably was, Andersen said. Some 40 years ago, when the county tried to straighten a jog at the intersection, the road caved in, creating a hole about 30 feet deep – which the county filled back in.

Still, one person who still thinks of the town often is Colley, the jazz musician who grew up in California and began studying the bass at age 11. He has toured with the likes of jazz vocal legend Carmen McRae, as well as Dizzy Gillespie and John Scofield.

Colley said he knows of no living connections to Empire. He knows through his Uncle Harry, who passed away two years ago, that a few of his relatives are buried in the Empire Cemetery, a site donated more than 130 years ago by Joseph Colby.

It's a site he's seen only in pictures.

"It would be great for me to be able to visit and explore the area around Galva," he said.

❖❖❖

A marker for the Sante Fe Trail is seen along 22nd Avenue, south of Galva.

Mennonite villages

❖ Marion County ❖

Mennonite settlement now seen by stone markers, tree rows and cemeteries

Tall, barren prairie lay in every direction. Not a sound stirred, except for the wind amid the grasses and the insects that swarmed.

Jacob Wiebe, his family and a number of other Mennonites had traveled from southern Russia to the Kansas plains where they sought religious freedom among the other pioneers just settling the nearly 15-year-old state. They had decided to leave the green fields of the Crimea forever and sought Kansas because the new state had similar soils to their native country - a good place to grow wheat. The group purchased a tract of land in central Kansas from the Santa Fe Railroad.

So, amid a hot August in 1874, Wiebe and congregation leaders traveled the uninhabited landscape 14 miles from Peabody to an area of Marion County.

"We rode in the deer grass to the little stake that marked the spot I had chosen. When we reached the spot, I stopped. My wife asked me, 'Why do you stop?' I said, 'We are to live here.' Then she began to weep."

Wiebe wrote the story as part of an essay 40 years later. For the woman, it must have seemed daunting to begin building a home on the lonely landscape - far from her native homeland, far from any settlement, said area historian Karen Penner after reading the marker that tells Wiebe's tale of settling the plains in 1874.

"It must have been overwhelming," Penner said.

Determined, however, these settlers had optimism for their future, she said. They named their new home Gnadenau, or Meadow of Grace.

Little villages on the prairie

Gnadenau was just the forefront of a large number of Mennonite settlements in south-central Kansas nearly 140 years ago - ghost villages now marked only by stone markers, tree rows and cemeteries.

The Mennonites first migrated from Europe to Russia under Catherine the Great for religious freedom. Nevertheless, 100 years later, changes took place under Alexander II impacting their beliefs. This included a universal military service act requiring the peaceful group to fight.

Thus, by the end of 1874, the first arrival of Mennonites, roughly 1,900 people, settled an area that consisted of 60,000 acres of land in Marion, McPherson, Harvey and Reno counties, according to a June 1973 article in Mennonite Life.

Also, some of the hard winter wheat that has made Kansas the breadbasket of the nation reached that state in the baggage of these immigrants from the steppes of southern Russia.

At first, the settlers were determined to retain the village tradition and pattern of farmland distribution they had had in Russia, according to the publication, Penner said.

Settlements like Gnadenau were set up like these Russian villages with long streets and several small farmsteads spaced evenly apart in a row along the street. Typically, in the middle of this long block was a school. Some villages also had a gristmill for processing the wheat the families brought with them.

Families were given nearby strips of land to tend.

Gnadenau, one of the first of more than a dozen villages settled in Marion and surrounding counties, was the largest of these villages. The village became the new home of 34 families, or 164 people, according to the Mennonite Life article.

Marion County. DEAD TOWNS. 15. 56. Hillsboro. Marion. 15. Mennonite villages. 50. 77.

At Gnadenau, a church was built, then a store and a couple of blacksmith shops. Jacob Friesen and his son operated a large gristmill west of the village, the publication stated.

Other villages had ethic names like Schoenthal, or Fair Valley in English; Gruenfeld, or Greenfield; and Hoffungsthal, which means Hope Valley.

All these villages were put into two communities, in essence, the Alexanderwhol and Krimmer Mennonite communities, according to the Mennonite publication. The Alexanderwhol community was the largest and consisted of eight villages in all.

The village setup lasted just three years before it was abandoned - due to confusion in paying taxes and because families

Mennonite villages

wanted personal property and independence, according to the publication. The Gnadenau village, however, lasted several more years before it became a ghost village.

"With the American system of private-land ownership, some moved out of the villages sooner," said Peggy Goertzen, director of the Center for Mennonite Brethren Studies at Tabor College in Hillsboro.

However, she said, "You can still see (village locations) and, at Hochfeld, you can still see the village pattern."

Family roots

On a spring day in 2011, Penner, a historian and board member with Newton's Bernhard Warkentin House - the man who helped bring Mennonites to Kansas - toured many of the former village sites.

A large green sign marks Hochfeld where tree rows still outline the village. A mile to the north is Springfield, which also is marked by a sign and a cemetery. At Alexanderfeld, there is a cemetery, as well as a church, school and stone pillar.

Meanwhile, at Gnadenau, a stone still marks the spot of where a cemetery once was located. Penner said most of the graves, as well as the church, were moved west to another site.

That church burned down several years ago and a new one

The stone marker at Gnadenau shows where 34 families settled in 1874. Besides farmsteads, Gnadenau had a store, gristmill and a school. Villages, however, are different than an actual town.

was built in Hillsboro, she said.

Hillsboro also has a full-sized replica of the wind-powered gristmill built in 1876 at Gnadenau on display.

Penner grew up around the Ebenfeld Mennonite Brethren Church area in Marion County near the town of Aulne. In June, she and her family gathered for a reunion at Bethel College, which included talking about their roots.

Eventually, she said, the family will erect a gravestone for her great grandmother, Adelgunda Penner Suderman Dueck, who died in 1888. She was buried with a couple of family members in a field near the Alexanderfeld community - a common practice back then. The family moved the grave to the Gnadenau cemetery in the 1970s but never put a marker on the plot, she said.

The family is beginning to raise money to mark her grave.

Family, after all, is important, she said.

"There is a saying that for your children to have wings they must have roots," she said. "And, to know where you are going in life, you have to know where you came. That has been my philosophy. I just like to learn the stories of who these people were, what they went through. That is what makes it fun for me – finding they were real people – not just a name and a date."

❖❖❖

A sign is placed at where the Mennonite settlement of Hochfeld was located in about 1874. These settlements or villages lasted about three years before residents dispersed to their own farms.

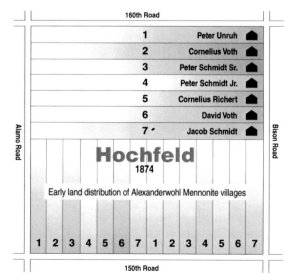

Aulne

❖ Marion County ❖

*Once considered for the location of Tabor College,
little Aulne is just a stop in the road.*

Karen Penner sometimes wonders what Aulne would have been like if the vote had gone the other way.

On this spring day, she stood amid the town's main drag with Hillsboro High School classmate Eugene Just. Brush and trees cover an area where businesses once stood – old stores that have long been carted off.

Along with a dozen or so houses, only the Methodist church still stands where area residents gather each Sunday. Catty-corner across the street is the old Aulne State Bank, which, on this day, is buzzing with a colony of bees. It hasn't been a lending institution in nearly 90 years – not since the banker embezzled money.

However, go back more than 100 years, when this little stop in the road had about 200 people and the region's Mennonite community was looking for a place to put up a college.

Because it was a town along the railroad, Aulne was one of the finalists. But, obviously, there is no college in this ghost town. Since 1908, Tabor College has resided in Hillsboro, a town with nearly 3,000 in population.

"Once upon a time, Aulne was probably bigger than Hillsboro," Penner said, adding that with the college, "Aulne would have been much different."

Little town in Marion County

In 1987, more than 1,100 people flocked to the streets of Aulne to celebrate its 100 years of existence.

It's also probably the last time so many people have been in the town at once. Founded in 1887 in Marion County, the area had residents for nearly 15 years before it officially became a city. Locals built a school as early as 1872. This was followed by a church a few years later, according to the book "Marion County, Kansas, Past and Present."

In 1887, a town company platted a community with residents, suggesting the name Brownsville in honor of O.C. Brown, one of the first settlers. That name, however, had already been taken, so they asked a railroad worker who was helping put in the railroad line his name. He answered Aulne, according to former resident Ellen Darrow, who chronicled the history for the centennial celebration.

Thus, Aulne was born – a town that, during its beginnings, had a mercantile, a cream station, barber, harness shop and blacksmiths. One family operated a restaurant and another served meals and rented rooms, Darrow said. There was a

depot and stockyards near the tracks to ship livestock. Farmers hauled their grain to the local elevator and, in 1907, entrepreneurs built a flourmill that began milling "Ideal Flour." The mill was discontinued in 1912 or 1913.

The town continued to flourish in 1914 when a reporter from the Topeka Capital visited it, according to the Marion County book. In fact, that year, the largest mercantile – Aulne Mercantile Co. – had four clerks and did $34,000 in sales. Business probably remained stable for several years after the visit and, in 1927, at least 10 businesses were still in Aulne, including two groceries, a bank, a service station, garage and a music and radio store.

Like other towns, Aulne had its share of problems, Darrow reported. That included tragic deaths. For instance, one man crawled between the cars of a train that suddenly jerked, causing him to fall beneath the wheels and lose his life.

An outbreak of typhoid fever in 1926 took one life and caused illness for others. It was thought the fever was caused by a contaminated water well used by a man who sold milk to various families in the town.

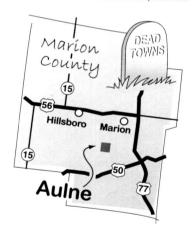

Location: Aulne is at the intersection of 140th Road and Pawnee Road in Marion County.

In addition, in the early 1900s, a little boy drowned in wheat in one of the wheat bins in the elevator.

The Aulne State Bank opened in 1909 but closed sometime in the 1920s after the banker, V.O. Johnson, pleaded guilty to embezzlement, according to The Hutchinson News. Johnson served time in prison. Other robberies occurred during the time before the bank shut down for good.

As the Great Depression hit and residents began driving to bigger cities to do business, things began to go downhill for Aulne. One by one, businesses closed and, by 1942, the lumberyard, two mercantile stores and several houses were sold and moved away, according to Darrow.

The school closed for good in the 1960s. It eventually was torn down. By the 1970s, just 35 people were still living in town.

Still home

Penner said she has fond memories of Aulne – from buying penny candy at the mercantile to watching her father go off with the other men for the annual New Year's Day coyote hunt. She and classmate Just both were employed for a time at the local elevator, which no longer exists. There were clubs, as well, including the Anti-Horse Thief Association, which sponsored an annual picnic and ball games, Just said.

"Stealing horses was as bad as robbing a bank," Just said.

Just stepped through the bank's threshold onto the wooden floor inside, which is still strong enough to support several people. He joked a resident once tried to make it a drive-

Eugene Just shows the interior of the Aulne State Bank, one of the remaining buildings in Aulne.

through bank after the man rammed into the front of the building with his vehicle.

At one time, it was even joked about around town that "Aulne is the only little town with a bank that is open 24 hours a day and on Sundays, too," because, for a time, the old structure had broken out windows and the door was ajar.

Just covered the opening, however, hoping to preserve the building a little while longer. At present, it's used for storage for the Methodist church, which Just attends. The church is one of the last relics bringing residents to town each Sunday, he said as he watched the train cross the tracks just up the road.

Darrow wrote for Aulne's centennial in 1987 that while Aulne is no longer a busy trading in center, residents here still take pride in their little town.

"Young propel and the ones living in Aulne area to be commended for keeping the town 'on the map,'" Darrow writes. "Who knows? Maybe it will last another 100 years."

"My Home Town"

I've traveled east and I've traveled west,
Now I'll tell you what I like the best –
It's coming back to my home town
Where people never let you down.

They are friendly folk who band together
To help each other in all kinds of weather.
The town has dwindled to very small,
But to me, it's the greatest little city of all.

The small towns and the villages
That are strewn across our land
Are the backbone of our nation,
Symbol of freedom, may she ever stand.

To build this town and community,
Brave pioneers strived without renown
So we honor them, in our hearts today,
Long live Aulne! It's "My Home Town."

-Ellen Darrow
July 1987

THE AULNE STATE BANK '09

Photos by Amy Bickel/The Hutchinson News

Karen Penner and Eugene Just stand outside the Aulne State Bank in Aulne. The town of Aulne was founded in 1887 in Marion County and was named after a railroad worker who was helping put in the railroad line.

RAVANNA! The Future County Seat of Garfield Co. A Real Town Backed by Unlimited Wealth! A Future City! The Place to Invest!

– from 1885 flyers and ads promoting the town of Ravanna

Amy Bickel/The Hutchinson News

Ruins of the Garfield County Courthouse still stand in a pasture in Ravanna. The courthouse was never used, as Garfield was declared an illegal county. The structure burned at the turn of the 20th century.

"If that railroad would have come through, it might have made the difference."

– Guy Reed , Finney County rancher, 2010